Writing Your Way
CREATING A PERSONAL JOURNAL

Writing Your Way

Creating a Personal Journal

by

Ellen Jaffe

SUMACH PRESS

CANADIAN CATALOGUING IN PUBLICATION DATA
Jaffe, Ellen, 1945-
Main entry under title:
Writing your way: creating a personal journal
Includes bibliographical references.
ISBN 1-894549-04-X

1. Diaries – Authorship. 2. Diaries – Therapeutic use.
3. Creative writing I. Title
PN4390.J33 2001   808'.06692   C2001-930152-9

Copyright © 2001 Ellen Jaffe

Edited by Gilda Mekler
Copy edited by Beth McAuley
Cover & Design by Liz Martin

Printed in Canada

Published by

SUMACH PRESS

1415 Bathurst Street, Suite 202
Toronto ON Canada M5R 3H8
sumachpress@on.aibn.com

www.sumachpress.com

DEDICATION

To my mother, Viola Jaffe,
My late father, Harry L. Jaffe,
And my son, Joe Bitz,

For their love, steadfast encouragement, and joie de vivre

Love and Thanks always

And to the Children, now Adults, in the writing group
"The Voice of the Children," led by poet June Jordan and teacher
Terri Bush: working with this group helped me see
how writing can change the world.

THE COVER: A NOTE ABOUT QUILTS

Not all stories are told on paper. Women have long been quilters. In quilting bees and circles, women meet together, not only to work but also to talk about their lives, or simply feel comfortable being together. The patterns on the quilts tell different stories, and the crazy quilt, made up of remnants — a wedding dress here, Grandpa's old shirt there — is a metaphor for life: all the bits and pieces of cloth hold memories of events and experiences in a seemingly chaotic pattern that blends together.

Quilts also serve as a medium of communication. I was fascinated to discover that in the southern United States, before the Civil War, African slaves used quilts to create a coded language that helped them escape to freedom along the Underground Railroad. *Hidden in Plain View*, by Jacqueline L. Tobin and Raymond G. Dobard, tells the story of this quilt language. The homespun, everyday nature of the quilts covered up their secrets.

Quilts carried messages in several ways: patterns, fabrics, colours and stitching. Displaying a quilt in a window, on a clothesline, even on graves in a cemetery indicated whether conditions were safe for escape, its pattern giving a certain message. The Monkey-Wrench pattern, for example, might be used to tell the slaves to gather tools and possessions for an escape; various star patterns directed them to follow the stars as they travelled north at night. The Dresden Plate pattern probably referred to Dresden, Ohio, and to Dresden in southwestern Ontario, a centre for newly freed slaves. In addition, the patterns were bright, lively and beautiful. Many of the designs were based on symbols from tribal Africa, brought over in memory on the slave-ships.

This story of quilts shows people's capacity to use whatever they have on hand in their search for dignity, freedom and meaning. Working stitch by stitch, the quilters gave each other directions and began taking direction and control over their own lives, passing on their stories from one generation to the next. In our writing, we also hope to take our lives into our own hands and change the world. We weave webs of words, of thoughts, of song, to keep off the cold.

Contents

Acknowledgements *9*

Starting Point
Introduction and Intention *13*
How to Use this Book *22*
Barriers and Pathfinders to Writing *26*

East
Language *41*
Who Am I? *56*
Beginnings *62*
Food and Clothing *65*
Landscape and Sense of Place *69*

South
Talking to Your Body *77*
Sexuality and the Erotic *86*
Children *93*
Animals *99*

West
Emotions *107*
Trauma *116*
Dreams *125*
Treats and Secrets *129*

North

Solitude and Loneliness *135*
Silence *140*
Death *148*
Spirituality *155*

The Circle of Time

Past *163*
Future *172*
Present *177*

Opening Doors

"Everything Else" *185*

References *197*
Further Reading *204*
Permissions *206*

Acknowledgements

In addition to the people mentioned in the dedication, I would like to thank the following:

Beth McAuley of Sumach Press, for her initial belief in this project, and her steady support along the way. Lois Pike and Liz Martin, also of Sumach, for their ongoing help. Gilda Mekler, editor and friend, whose invaluable insight and hard work helped the book find its own direction. Dr. Naomi June Diamond, for her inspired teaching, love of literature and sharp eye for writing.

All the women of the Feminist Women's Writing Workshops (Geneva, New York). The women in the Women's Work Writing Workshop in Hamilton, for welcoming me into their group and providing a home base for writing: Sharon Bray, Dawn Sabire, Angela Hrabowiak (who also read part of the manuscript), Morgan Combes, Susan Evans Shaw, Linda Marie Fulcher, Kathleen Moore, Marian Cawley, and Renee Sagebear. Special thanks to Renee for creating and running The Women's Bookstop in Hamilton and for encouraging creativity in the women's community.

Lil Blume, James Deahl, April Severin and other Hamilton writers, including members of Gallery 435, for their encouragement and support; Gertrude Lebans and Ann Turner of artemis enterprises; Linda Palmer and Rosemary Duffy, for discussing ideas in early stages; and CRIAW (The Canadian Research Institute for the Advancement of Women), at whose conference in 1999 I presented a workshop which germinated the idea for this book.

All the students and teachers with whom I have worked over the years for sharing their lives and their words. Particular thanks to Sandy Hill (principal) and Paula Laing (teacher), Emily C. General Public School, Six Nations Reserve, Ohsweken. I am also grateful to Bernadette Wabie (public education officer) and Winnie Jacobs (librarian) of the Woodland Cultural Centre, and to Sandra Montour of Ganohkwa Sra Family Assault Support Services at Six Nations.

I acknowledge the writers whose work I have read and loved over the years, especially the writers I have discovered and rediscovered while working on this book. I am grateful to those who have given me permission to use their work.

✽

Starting Point

*Cultivate in your work and in your life
the art of patience, and come to terms
with your inevitable human limitations
while striving to extend the boundaries
of your understanding, your knowledge
and your compassion.*

> — MARGARET LAURENCE
> from the Historical Plaque
> placed in front of her home in
> Lakefield, Ontario by the Lakefield
> Historical Society

INTRODUCTION AND INTENTION

> Ultimately, a poem has an electrical force-field, which is love.
>
> — Joy Harjo, in *The Language of Life*

"YOU'RE WRITING A BOOK about writing?" asks a woman who lives down the street, someone I've met through Neighbourhood Watch. "The only thing I've ever wanted to write about was the neighbours next door — the old couple there," she says. "They're dead now, but they helped me a lot when I was younger. His wife and I would have a cup of tea and tell the same stories, twenty times or more — but they were always a little bit different."

Another friend says, "I don't want to be a *writer* — but I want to write down the stories I have in my head." Over coffee, she is telling me a story about her mother and her grandmother, almost forgotten but called to mind by an item in today's newspaper.

This is a book to help you write those stories and poems you have always wanted to write, and to let you discover stories you didn't know you knew. The text and exercises are directed towards women's experience, as this is an area that I know more about, and in which I think women need to be encouraged. But many of the exercises could also be done by men. My philosophy about writing applies to anyone.

I want to show you that creative writing can do several things: help you heal from trauma and the buffeting of daily

Starting Point

life; live a freer, more compassionate and playful life; and feel more connected to yourself, to other people and to the natural and spiritual world. Further, I think each of us has the ability to write in her own way, though some people become professional writers and others do not. Putting writers on a pedestal can devalue the more universal human desire to express ourselves in language. A certain ability and love of language, plus dedication, commitment, energy and focus, make a writer — but that does not make writing off limits to other people. Not everyone is Marnie McBean or Wayne Gretzky, but many people row or play hockey. Let's focus on the verb, not the noun: not on being a *writer*, but on *writing*.

And the interesting thing is that, sometimes, writing often and with commitment causes a shift in attitude and you may realize you are a writer, after all.

You can use writing in many ways. The personal journal that you create can take various forms; it can be a letter, memoir, poem, a play or a children's story, or any other genre.

Let's look again at my friend's statement, "The stories were a little bit different each time." There is never a right or wrong way to tell a story. If it changes, perhaps telling it twice — or twenty times — has made us remember something new, or an incident in daily life has shed new light on the story.

Something as simple as a smell or a taste may evoke long-forgotten memories, as in the famous example of Marcel Proust dipping a piece of cake into his linden tea and rediscovering his childhood. Stories, like cakes, have many layers — you may need to tell one story to find the one hiding beneath it.

Sometimes we search for exact details, whether the story is fiction or taken from real life; we need to know the year, even the day, a certain event happened, or whether a certain building existed in 1932. At other times, we can stretch the truth or embroider it. Ruth Reichl says in her memoir, *Tender at the Bone*, "Storytelling, in my family, was highly prized ... The good stories, of course, were repeated endlessly until they took on a

INTRODUCTION AND INTENTION

life of their own ... This book is absolutely in the family tradition. Everything here is true, but it may not be entirely factual." Dayal Kaur Khalsa begins her children's story *Tales of a Gambling Grandma* by telling us how her grandmother came to America from Russia in a hay cart, wearing only one shoe, "at least, that's how she told the story to me."

In "On Poetry," American poet Marianne Moore gave a definition that has become famous: poetry is "imaginary gardens with real toads in them." This vivid image shows how the two worlds of imagination and actuality weave together to make a story or poem. *Poetry* itself comes from Greek and Indo-European roots which mean "make, construct, arrange." And *story* comes from a word meaning "vision." So in writing we are making and recreating an arrangement of the world, using what we see, experience and imagine.

Writing itself is a journey which we take step by step. Each of us writes in her own way, her own manner, but the process of writing can also help you *find your way*, guiding you along the tangled paths of life. Writing is often a journey whose end we do not know: I begin a poem, story or journal entry with an idea, an image, a voice, a feeling, but then it takes its own direction and I have to listen and follow, maybe push some overgrown bushes aside, to see what is happening.

E.L. Doctorow has said that "writing a novel is like driving a car at night. You can only see as far as your headlights, but you can make the entire journey that way." Add to this scene some fog, or headlights not working or not being sure which road to take. But then you find yourself, at dawn, in a valley you've never seen before but where you feel at home.

When I first thought about choosing a title for this book, I was inspired by the fairy tale *East of the Sun, West of the Moon*. In this story, a young woman has to take many arduous journeys, in the directions of the four winds (south, west, east and north) before being reunited with her true love. In folk tales and legends, the struggle to find one's true love is often a symbol for

Starting Point

finding and loving oneself, for becoming whole. The heroine has the courage to face her past mistakes and fears and move on with her life. This is, I believe, something that writing can help you achieve.

I liked the idea of travelling in the directions of the compass we use every day and also through time (past, present and future) to find a place where creativity, magic and insight may happen. And I liked being able to return from that place to our daily lives, enriched and more aware, carrying some of that magic with us. There is a Chinese saying that there are five directions: north, south, east, west and *here*.

I hope this book will help you travel more surely in both worlds and be intrigued by the links between them. More and more, I think that "east of the sun, west of the moon" is not a place but a *state of mind* we can find anywhere.

In choosing the title, *Writing Your Way*, I want to emphasize the idea of each reader/writer finding her own way in the world we all share. In many cultures, including those of Native America, the four directions have symbolic as well as practical meanings and are part of the Sacred Tree or Medicine Wheel holding the world together. In these beliefs, North and South, East and West are not isolated entities, but are connected by axis lines that link them to each other and to the circle of life. Teachings of various Native and Aboriginal nations talk about the need to make a journey *around* the directions, so that we may become whole. This is a journey we take over and over again through life, in many different ways. Shamans from cultures around the world summon the four directions when performing healing ceremonies, to add both natural and sacred power to the occasion.

I found that "journal" is related to the word "journey." Both derive from the French word jour, "day." This word traces its roots back to Latin *diurnal*, "daily," from *dies*, "daylight." I was surprised to find that it shares an ultimate root with *divine* and *Diana*, Latin version of the Greek Artemis, the virgin moon

INTRODUCTION AND INTENTION

goddess, through the word *deus*, "god" and "godlike." They all derive from a Sanskrit word meaning "shining." At the same time, creativity is also connected to the earth, to the darkness of night and underground, and to the processes of nurturing, dying and new growth.

I have tried to choose topics for discussion and writing that correspond, at least loosely, to the symbolic meanings of the directions. Various cultures interpret these directions in different ways: for example, water is connected with the south in one tradition, with the west in another. I have chosen a common schema that feels comfortable to me. The important thing is that, in moving around the directions, we encounter each of the four elements — fire, water, earth and air — and the four aspects of human nature — body, emotions, mind and spirit.

But why write? Why not just go on living, as well as possible? Consider this poem:

> Last night, as I was sleeping
> I dreamt — marvellous error! —
> that I had a beehive
> here inside my heart,
> And the golden bees
> were making white combs
> and sweet honey
> from my old failures.
>
> — ANTONIO MACHADO
> from *Times Alone*,
> translated by Robert Bly

The last line catches the heart. Writing cannot undo or change the past but, like the work of bees, it can initiate an imaginative transformation, turning "old failures" into "white combs and sweet honey."

This is not done casually or easily. It takes a combination of dream, intention, grace and hard work. Writing puts us in a place where transformation happens. Like the ancient

Starting Point

alchemists, we do not discard the lead of life, but turn it into gold, into the philosopher's stone.

The act of writing is, I believe, healing, whether we write about seemingly small daily events or large issues. Writing about the minutiae of daily life validates their importance. And sometimes, as we write about it, a seemingly trivial event will open a window into feelings or events that have puzzled us for years.

Even when we are writing about painful things, the act of writing, of creating — putting thoughts, feelings and images into words — is deeply healing and affirming.

Often, we find we are writing about something we thought we had dealt with long ago. These important events may spiral around in our lives, so we are not back at the same place, but on another level of the spiral. Psychotherapist Yvonne Dolan uses the analogy of falling and cutting your knee on broken glass — you wash your knee carefully and clean out most of the glass, but even years later, a few small slivers still emerge, one at a time.

This metaphor reminds me of the evil mirror in Hans Christian Anderson's story "The Snow Queen," which breaks and falls on the world. Tiny slivers get stuck in people's eyes and, even worse, in their hearts. People cannot prevent these slivers from being there, but the task of healing is to become aware of them and then remove them, as much as possible.

The opposite version of this cosmic mirror appears as the epigram of Adele Wiseman's novel *Crackpot:* she cites the Kabbalistic (Jewish mystical) legends of creation, in which the Divine Light is stored in a vessel but the vessel is unable to contain this light and bursts; its shards, imbued with sparks of this holy light, scatter throughout the universe.

Writing can be an act of re-membering (putting back together), and also of stretching, expanding, taking us to that place east of the sun and west of the moon without leaving the kitchen table. It takes us beyond experience and belief into imagination and narrative, the place of Open Sesame. It can

INTRODUCTION AND INTENTION

also help us see things from the point of view of the *other*, whether this is another person, ourselves at another time or even animals and nature. Margaret Mahler, a child psychologist, talks about the toddler who "has a love affair with the world." I think writers feel this way too, even when writing in anger and sorrow.

I'll close this introduction with another personal story. A couple of years ago, I stopped at a restaurant on my way back from a writing workshop. The waitress, named Kimberly (I could see by her name tag), asked about the book I was reading. When I told her that it was written by a friend of mine, she asked if I was also a writer, and I said yes. (A few years earlier, I would not have been able to say that.)

"I used to write too," she confided. "I had notebooks of stories, thirty, forty pages. But the more I read, it seemed all the good plots were taken."

I suggested there might be only a few plots in the world, but everyone could write about them in her own way. "Put on their own personal touches, you mean?" she asked, seeing the situation in a new light. "Do you think I should try again?"

"Definitely," I told her.

Kimberly's voice kept haunting me on the drive home, and I wrote a monologue in her voice: "This woman came into the restaurant today, sat at a table for one. She was reading this book ... " It ended with Kimberly signing up for a creative writing class, despite misgivings about what her boyfriend Wayne would think. I have no idea, of course, if she ever did this, or if she had a boyfriend Wayne: thus is fiction born from real life. I do know that she used to write, got discouraged, wanted to try again.

I could hear Kimberly's voice, and I was interested in her feelings about writing. I wanted to write a book that would help Kimberly get started again. I have also met teachers who aren't sure how to help their students with creative writing, and people who write reports and notes as part of their work, but are hesitant to write about their own feelings and experiences. On a bus from Hamilton to Toronto, I talked with a retired nurse who said, with tears in her eyes, that she had never been taught English well at school; what little she knew came from her Latin teacher. This book is for all these women.

At first, I saw myself as different from Kimberly. But as I read a variety of books about writing, both familiar and new, and began the writing work myself, I found something holding back my pen. Like Kimberly, I had my own version of "all the good plots are taken." Despite encouragement from my editor and my friends, I found myself thinking: "People who are wiser and better writers than I am have written books about writing. What more do I have to add? What's the point of writing this book? Will anyone want to read it?"

This is the voice of discouragement, self-doubt and fear that every writer faces, with every new blank page. While it is important to evaluate your work honestly, this Inner Critic is, I think, a false voice, coming from our own fears or absorbed from family, teachers and friends as we grew up. "Why waste your time doing that?" "Scribbling again?" "Why don't you do something important?" We take in these voices and play them back in our minds at high volume, drowning out the self who whispers, "Listen to me. I have something to say, too!"

We will look this Inner Critic in the eye in the chapter on Barriers and, throughout the book, discover ways to disarm her (or him). As Bonni Goldberg says in *Room to Write*, you gain strength by affirming yourself in the face of this critic; it's like strengthening your muscles by exercising with weights on.

INTRODUCTION AND INTENTION

EXERCISE

1. *When I Sit Down to Write ...*

This is an exercise that novelist Dorothy Allison suggested at a writing workshop. It is a good place to start. Settle yourself in a comfortable place, take out a notebook or turn on your computer, and write for ten minutes on what happens "When I Sit Down to Write." What distractions are there? What thoughts come, what fears, what hopes? How do you feel in your body? One woman in a workshop told me that when she began writing, she felt tense and had some trouble breathing, but she began to feel better and more relaxed as she continued working. This, like most of the exercises in this book, is one that can be done again and again, at different times in your life. It might be interesting to do it two or three times as you work through the book and again at the end — then compare all your versions.

✦

How to Use this Book

I say, Write
She say, Nothing but death can keep me from it.

— Alice Walker, *The Color Purple*

THIS BOOK IS MEANT TO BE INCLUSIVE in its readership. It is for women of all ages, sexual orientations, cultural or ethnic background and state of wellness. I have tried to shape the chapters and exercises so that they can be used in a variety of ways and can be accessible to women whose primary language is not English, or who have met with particular difficulties in their walk through the world. I have tried to provide enough choice or variation within each exercise so that women do not feel excluded for any reason. For example, there is an opportunity to write about a child or children, but these can be children you know or remember, whether related to you or not.

The next chapter looks at barriers to writing and strategies to get around them. Following this are four sections, each representing one of the four different directions of East, South, West and North; and a section representing the Circle of Time, made up of Past, Present and Future. Within each section are chapters that deal with themes relating to that direction or time and writing exercises to explore these themes and generate new ideas. The concluding chapter summarizes what we have done and opens the door to future writing. *Writing Your Way* is a sampler, a smorgasbord of various ideas. Each chapter could be

HOW TO USE THIS BOOK

expanded into a book in itself, but I hope they give you a taste of various things to write about, as well as ideas about writing techniques, language and creativity.

I hope that this book captures the flavour of a writing workshop. In the workshops I teach, I suggest and explain a topic or idea, but let each person approach it in her own way (or even write something completely different). I am often delighted, moved and surprised by what emerges. The idea is to surprise *yourself* with what you write. It is too easy to limit ourselves to the obvious, the superficial. Most of the exercises focus on content, but some suggest tools and techniques that explore and expand your use of words and language.

Because this is not a workbook, you will need to buy a notebook or a journal. Or you may prefer to write on the computer — whatever is most comfortable for you. As you continue writing, you may want to date your journals and keep them in a safe place, so you can refer to them later on.

You may want to start in the East (the usual place of beginning) and work your way around, or you may want to start with the section that interests or intrigues you most. You will see that the exercises begin with lighter, more accessible material and work towards deeper, perhaps harder, subjects in the West and North sections, then move around again to material that is perhaps more fun in the later chapters.

You can use this book to plan your journal writing in several ways. You can read one chapter a week and do all four exercises in each. Or you can read a chapter each day that you write and choose one of the exercises. Or you can read the whole book through and then go back and choose those exercises that call for you to write them. There is no wrong way, as long as you bring your experience and imagination to the writing exercises in this book and use them to work with your own needs and issues. The idea is to have fun, to make writing, in the words of children's author Sarah Ellis, not hard work but "hard play."

Starting Point

Individual women, women meeting together as a group, even women sharing their work on the Internet, can use *Writing Your Way*. It can add impetus to an ongoing writing group or be the basis for starting one. (We will look at starting and using writing groups at the close of the book.) The exercises can be adapted for use with various special groups, such as those connected to a hospital, shelter, school or seniors' centre.

I have tried to make this book both accessible and welcoming, so that you, the reader and my co-writer, will feel at home. As in a writing circle, I want to make it a safe place: not a place of uniformity or hiding but a place where diversity is respected and where each woman can write from her unique point of view.

The quotes and examples of writing used in the book are identified by author and title as they appear. Complete references are found in the bibliography. I have chosen primarily writing by women, as this book focuses on women's experience, but I've also included quotes by men that are relevant and that have been helpful to me.

My Background

I will share some of my background to introduce myself and to show what led to writing this book. I grew up in New York City and went to university at Wellesley College in Massachusetts. I lived briefly in California, and then longer in England, before coming to Canada in 1979. I have worked as a teacher and as a psychotherapist (including play therapy with children). From childhood on, I have always written poems, stories, plays, diaries. As the American poet Diane Wakoski has said about her life, I found it easier to write than to talk about my feelings, and then continued writing even when I could talk more easily. I began teaching writing in 1968 with The Voice of the Children, a group of Black and Hispanic children in Brooklyn, New York, led by poet June Jordan and teacher Terri Bush. In recent years, I have taught many writing workshops in schools across Ontario, sometimes sponsored by Artists in Education grants from the Ontario Arts Council or by the Learning Through the Arts program. I have also worked with women's groups and conferences. My interests in healing, myth and different cultures led me to study shamanic healing with Michael Harner, Sandra Ingerman and other members of the Foundation of Shamanic Studies, an organization which has developed a concept of core shamanism, based on work with people around the world.

I have published poems, stories and other writing, taken part in readings, and won some awards. Beyond this, I have found that writing is a centring force in my life, work and relationships.

※

Barriers and Pathfinders to Writing

Take one blank sheet ...
Take risks.

— Ellen Jaffe

WRITING IS TRIAL AND ERROR — or trial and trial and trial, going further and deeper each time. As I wrote this on my computer, I made the typographical error of *trial and terror*, which may be close to the truth. Sometimes going forward with our writing means going *fearward*, as Barbara Turner-Vessalgo says in the book *Freefall*. The area that feels fraught with fear, the place we want to avoid, is often the place we need to go and where the energy of the writing is leading.

But sometimes it is hard to get started. Before beginning this journey, we will look at some beliefs and ideas that are barriers to writing, and at strategies that can help us get around these barriers and find the right path.

1. BARRIER: *Writers need lots of free time to write. I have a job and a family, and just don't have that kind of time. Maybe I'll have to wait until I do — or not write at all.*

PATHFINDER: Writers also have busy lives, often with other jobs and family responsibilities. If you want to write for personal growth, you can choose the time that you want and need. Many people who write about writing agree that fifteen minutes a day is a good amount, especially if you can make it a daily practice and set that aside as your own special time. One woman I know began by writing just one line a day, but she did it every day. Eventually, your line might become a paragraph, and your fifteen minutes half an hour.

As women, we are accustomed to doing for others who become dependent on us, so even taking a short time each day for ourselves can seem selfish. We have to learn to nurture this selfishness and redefine it as self-love, which can replenish us and enhance our relationships with others. Just as on an airplane, people are advised to put on their own oxygen masks before helping children and other dependents, we have to put on the oxygen masks of our own creative spirit before nurturing others.

Novelist Adele Wiseman says that in choosing to "opt for everything, to be fully human beings and fully writers, women set themselves a truly more heroic task than do our men, for few of us have 'wives' and secretaries" to make life easier. (*Memoirs*, p. 53).

If possible, find the time during which you are least likely to be disturbed. This may be early in the morning, late at night or during your lunch hour. In an interview on CBC Radio, Carol Shields talked about how she combined writing with being a mother, at first writing during short periods while her children were at school and gradually making that time longer. Margaret Laurence, too, said that she wrote while her children were at school, giving herself a "re-entry phase" before they came home, so she could move from the world of the novel back to daily life.

Although this may be easier said than done, let your family, partner and friends know that you are writing and don't want to be disturbed. Lucy Maud Montgomery, for example, went into her room to write in the afternoons, and her small sons sometimes passed her notes through the closed door.

Julia Cameron, in her books *The Artist's Way* and *The Right to Write*, suggests doing "morning pages," three pages every morning, just letting your thoughts come as they will.

Starting Point

Sometimes this takes you to surprising places and also clears a path for the day ahead. The important thing is to find a time that will (usually) work for you. Workshop leader Kay Leigh Hagan suggests that if you miss several days or weeks, you can begin writing again by commenting briefly on why you stopped, and why you've restarted.

Most of the exercises in this book can be done in a fifteen-minute sitting, though you might want or need to work on some for more than one day.

2. BARRIER: *I need a special room to write in, a place where I can have complete privacy.*

PATHFINDER: Despite Virginia Woolf's famous statement that "a woman must have money and a room of her own if she is to write fiction," you can write anywhere if you have something you want to say. Ursula K. LeGuin notes that Harriet Beecher Stowe wrote *Uncle Tom's Cabin* at the kitchen table.

At home, try to find a place where you can keep your writing materials and a few books, pictures and other things that set the scene for you — perhaps a plant, a comfortable cushion, a special mug for tea or coffee.

Sometimes, you may decide to try writing away from home, in places like a coffee shop (at non-peak hours), a museum or a park. Or you may find yourself in a new place and want to do some writing while you are there. Some of the exercises in this book ask you to go outside to various places to do your writing. Travelling in a train or airplane, or being away from home on vacation, is a good time to experiment with different kinds of writing. Being in nature might lead you to write more reflectively or to look at the natural world in a new way. Away from home, our senses become more alert, more open, and we react to new people, places and situations. You may want to pick a character whom you meet on your travels (as I did with Kimberly), and write from that person's point of view.

Trips to see family or friends may be important occasions

for writing. Sometimes the dislocation of a trip, whether for business or pleasure, arouses new thoughts, feelings and impressions, and your writing can help you understand these.

Because the practice of writing is so portable, even if you use a computer some of the time, it's good to get into the habit of writing in longhand, keeping your pen or pencil moving across the page. Computers, however are wonderful for saving and revising your work, and make writing more accessible for people with physical challenges.

3. BARRIER: *Writers are depressed, often crazy, and I don't want to become like that. I have enough trouble holding my life together as it is; maybe writing will make things worse.*

PATHFINDER: Writers often write about subjects that are sad, tragic or angry — but this does not mean they themselves are always like that. This barrier relates to the belief that the writer, or artist, is a lonely genius, inspired at odd hours, or that she is like the madwoman in the attic inhabiting so many Victorian novels. But probably clinical depression and other mental illnesses are no more common in writers than in the population at large. Natalie Goldberg, Julia Cameron and other writers agree that exploring your feelings in language can actually help you keep sane and centred, less helpless and overwhelmed by circumstances. In later chapters, we will look more closely at why writing about something that makes you sad or angry can actually make you *less* unhappy and *more* resilient.

In the nineteenth-century story "The Yellow Wallpaper" by Charlotte Perkins Gilman, we see a young woman fall apart and slip into madness, partly *because* her husband and doctor prevent her from writing. The (nameless) heroine says:

> Personally, I believe that congenial work, with excitement and change, would do me good. But what is one to do? I did write for a while in spite of them; but it does exhaust me a good deal — having to be so sly about it, or else meet with heavy opposition.

Starting Point

You can help deal with stress as you begin to write (working your way through this book and continuing on your own) by finding support from various sources. These include other women writers and perhaps male writers too; friends and family when possible; and, when necessary, a counsellor or therapist, especially one who is comfortable with the creative writing process. As Julia Cameron notes in *The Right to Write*, writing can be therapeutic, but it is not therapy, and you may wish to work with a therapist if the writing evokes memories and feelings that are difficult to handle on your own.

My friend Maida Tilchen calls the people who support you "cheerleaders for your writing." They can encourage you and provide practical help; perhaps they can babysit or give you a journal on your birthday.

You can also keep notes *about* your writing, perhaps just a few lines at the end of each exercise noting how you felt about doing it, and whether the exercise evoked any particularly unsettling memories or emotions.

There are a few tricks to help you feel better after a stint of hard writing. Drinking a glass of water, perhaps with a slice of lemon in it, is cleansing and grounding. Going for a walk around the block, doing some yoga stretches, working in the garden or playing with your dog or cat are other good ways to get back into your body and the everyday world.

4. BARRIER: *People will read what I write, without my permission, or its opposite: no one will like what I write or want to read it.*

PATHFINDER: The first issue is one of privacy, and finding a safe place for your writing. In Carol Shields's novel *Swann: A Mystery*, the poet hides her poems under the kitchen linoleum, so her husband won't find them. I hope you are not living in such a precarious and intimidating situation, but if you are, perhaps you could keep your journal at work or in your handbag, at a friend's house or in another safe place. We may have memories of mothers or friends who read our diaries, but as an

BARRIERS AND PATHFINDERS TO WRITING

adult, you are entitled to write what you want and what you believe to be true, and to keep your writing private if you wish. Especially in a difficult situation, writing can be your ally in reflecting on and planning your life.

It is also important to remember that you are writing for yourself. No one else has to read it. This book is not about writing for publication: it's about writing for you. (In the last section "Opening Doors," I talk briefly about the revision process and various ways to share your work if you want to.) The thought that "No one will like what I write or want to read it" most likely comes from the voice of the Inner Critic, that voice patched together from remarks of teachers, parents and the deprecating voice of society, joining with our own fears and self-doubts. Kimberly, the waitress, probably had these voices blaring in her head at high volume — but she was willing to ask, "Should I try again?"

You are writing for yourself, first of all. You may begin sharing your work in a writing group or with a few friends or family members. They may be moved or delighted by what you've done and may also make a few constructive suggestions. You may be surprised to find that your work does communicate to other people. But when you sit down to write, pen in hand, try to write for your own eye and ear and mind, and be open to the positive energy that is there to listen without judging.

The belief that your writing may not be welcomed may possibly relate to the idea that *real* artists and writers are men. This sounds absurd now, but for some of us the idea that women's work is minor or unimportant may linger. Women have often been prevented from saying the things we want to say, and not listened to or taken seriously when we do say them; see, for instance, Joanna Russ's insightful study *How to Suppress Women's Writing*. From the mid-twentieth century onward, however, women's writing, especially in Canada, has been widely accepted and valued. In fact, many of Canada's most famous authors are women: Margaret Atwood, Alice Munro, Beth

Starting Point

Brant, Ann Carson, Gabrielle Roy, Dionne Brand ... the list could go on and on.

5. BARRIER: *Writing and the other arts are "a frill," not to be taken seriously. I'd be better off doing housework or volunteering for a worthwhile cause.*

PATHFINDER: You can, in fact, do all these things. But writing is something that touches us at a very deep level, as well as giving us pleasure, a necessary part of life. This complaint is another aspect of the Inner Critic and of a society that denies the importance of art as a way to get to the he*art* of things. Creativity is one of the qualities that makes us human.

We often understand more about a social or political situation from a poem, novel or play than from long factual reports: Dickens's novels about poor children are a popular example, but so are modern works like Joy Kogawa's *Obasan* and Tomson Highway's *Kiss of the Fur Queen*.

Writing and the other arts deal with matters of life and death and the spirit as well as social issues. Many Canadian writers are involved with International PEN, the organization that promotes freedom of writers around the world. In countries where writers are imprisoned and tortured, no one sees art as insignificant.

Sometimes characters themselves can strengthen our motivation. Emily of New Moon, a heroine of L.M. Montgomery's, is told by her Aunt Elizabeth not to write stories because they waste paper and, more important, they are "a wicked and sinful thing." Even Emily's Aunt Laura, usually more sympathetic, says, "It is not as if it was anything that mattered much — it is really a waste of time." Emily responds ardently: "I *have* to go on writing stories, even though I am so very sorry you disapprove."

6. BARRIER: *Writing is only for people with talent, and I don't have that kind of talent, or even education. I'm not even good at spelling and grammar.*

BARRIERS AND PATHFINDERS TO WRITING

PATHFINDER: Everyone is born with the ability to communicate, and most of us learn a language well enough to speak and write. Skills in grammar, spelling and form can be learned and developed as you go on. English is a particularly hard language to spell because words come from many linguistic roots, so we have many homonyms (words like through and threw; to, too and two). Wanting to write your own story can motivate you to learn more about reading and writing, and books about writing, like this one, can demystify the process. As in most activities, the more you do it, the better you will be and the more you will find your own voice. Remember that this isn't school and no one is grading you. As David McFadden writes:

> In the finest writing there's a magic
> that will outlive marble and the fame of tyrants,
> and in the most ordinary writing, if honest,
> there's a seed of magic that grows and grows
> and blossoms with time ...
> "The Night Watchman," *The Art of Darkness*

7. BARRIER: *My life is boring, there's nothing to write about.*

PATHFINDER: The idea is not to be sensational or new, but to write about your own life in your unique way. Beginning writers are often advised "Write about what you know." I would say yes — and no. We "know" what we know in different ways. You may know about a community on an unnamed planet, or how a tree feels when it is being cut down. The novelist Henry James said that a writer could base a whole novel on a conversation overheard on the stairs. On the other hand, writing about familiar things means that you have to know them in a new way. Instead of taking them for granted, look at these things with new eyes. The poet Samuel Taylor Coleridge talked about "making the familiar strange, and the strange familiar."

Here is a poem about the writing process that starts with familiar things. The title comes from the street address where

Starting Point

my writing group met for several years; Linda Marie plays with the happy coincidence of the name of the street and its meaning for our work. (One trick of writing is to use what's on hand. If the street had been Homewood, Locke or Prospect, she could have used that. Names like Herkimer or Bloor aren't as symbolic, but then, she might have found another image.) Linda Marie begins with the home itself and the women gathered around a table, but in the second verse of the poem, she sees this familiar place in a new, more symbolic way.

CLIFF AVENUE

A wooden table, fresh cut flowers
    pens and paper,
water, tea and wine;
the gathering of women
to share our love of language
    and write.

We run and dive over the cliff
    into the topic
and the words flow out;
like wings we spread them
to catch the winds of our emotion
    and fly.

Exercising the power to name:
    roses in full bloom
and the iridescent dragonfly;
experiences of birth, love, sex, death
to record the stories of our lives, first hand,
    and read.

— Linda Marie, June 2000, unpublished

This poem really does encourage us to fly, to take the risk of leaping over the cliff in the company of trusted friends, and to name what we know, who we are.

BARRIERS AND PATHFINDERS TO WRITING

I'll close with the words of Ursula K. LeGuin, a wise woman of the writer's craft. In her essay, "The Fisherwoman's Daughter," a little girl asks:

> "Tell me, Auntie. What is the one thing a writer has to have?"
>
> "I'll tell you," says the imagination. "The one thing a writer has to have is not balls. Nor is it a child-free space. Nor is it even, speaking strictly on the evidence, a room of her own, though that is an amazing help, as is the goodwill and cooperation of the opposite sex, or at least the local, in-house representative of it. But she doesn't have to have that. The one thing a writer has to have is a pencil and some paper. That's enough, so long as she knows that she and she alone is in charge of that pencil, and responsible, she and she alone, for what it writes on the paper. In other words, that she's free. Not wholly free. Never wholly free. Maybe very partially. Maybe only in this one act, this sitting for a snatched moment being a woman writing, fishing the mind's lake. But in this, responsible; in this, autonomous; in this, free."
>
> "Auntie," says the little girl, "can I go fishing with you now?"

— From *Dancing at the Edge of the World*, p. 236

Starting Point

EXERCISES

1. *Getting a Journal*

Take the time to find or buy a writing notebook and pens. There are many kinds of notebooks and journals available, so find one that appeals to you. Try the dollar store or sidewalk sales. Decorate your notebook in whatever way you would like. Decide where you will keep this book and what time of day you would most like to use it. Write a dedication or intention (a mission statement) for your book; "In this book, I will ... And I hope to ..."

2. *Colours of My Mind: A Warm-up*

The world around us is full of colours, to which we have our own associations. These can be personal or cultural; the colours of weddings and mourning, for example, vary around the world. A colour can suggest something in the outside world — red could make you think of a cardinal or of your favourite sweater, for example — or a feeling, like love or anger. A colour might even suggest a sound or a smell.

Write down three different colours, leaving a space of several lines between each, and then describe what each colour makes you think of and how it makes you feel. There are two ways of doing this:

> 1) list at least four things each colour makes you think of. These can be anything at all. For example:
> *Blue:* forget-me-nots, blue jays in the garden, my son's old blue blanket, Bessie Smith, singing the blues.

> 2) list one item for each of the five senses, plus an emotion. For example:
> Red is the sight of a rose in bloom
> the sound of a cardinal singing
> the smell of fresh strawberries

INTRODUCTION AND INTENTION

>   the taste of hot peppers
>   the touch of velvet
>   the emotion of love, or of anger.

This can be a fifteen-minute timed writing.

3. *Cheerleaders (without the pom-poms!)*

Who are some "cheerleaders for your writing" or for your life in general? Describe one, and why this person's support is important to you and why the support makes you come alive. If you can't think of anyone to fill this role, make up a personal ad for a (writing) cheerleader, listing the qualities you would like. Of course, you won't put this ad in the local paper, but you may find you meet a few qualified candidates just by writing it. A strong intention can sometimes bring itself into being.

4. *Audre Lorde wrote, "I am not only a casualty, I am also a warrior."*
>   ("The Transformation of Silence into Language and Action,"
>   *Sister Outsider*, p. 41)

How does this statement apply to your life? Do you agree with it? Disagree? In one workshop, a woman told me that she did not feel that she was a casualty at all, and you may feel the same way. Write a paragraph about this statement as it applies to you and also one that applies to another woman you know — grandmother, mother, sister, friend, lover, mentor.

✽

East

Spring
Sunrise
Air
Beginnings ... the seed, the egg
Illumination, Clarity, Creativity
   Spirit soars towards the light

Spring, reluctant, slow
Found today beneath a stone
Whisper of green.

— GINA SHELTON
"Seasons"

LANGUAGE

> in writing
> poems,
> people-
> startling
> words
> come
> invisibly
>
> — Li Ch'ing-chao (1084-1151)

PEOPLE-STARTLING WORDS. Words that make us sit up and take notice — like the words in this short excerpt from a poem by a woman writing almost one thousand years ago. Perhaps they are words that people — especially women — are not supposed to say. Dirty words. Dangerous words. Silly words. Beautiful words. Unusual words. Words that shake us out of apathy, that open our senses.

Words are the writer's tools and need to be sharp. They are the main ingredients of the cake and need to be fresh. In this chapter, we will look at words themselves and at some ways to use them in your writing.

Words

In Alice Munro's short story "Spelling," Rose wonders about her aged stepmother's concept of words. The old woman can hardly speak and cannot see, but spells aloud the words that people say to her.

East

Were they like words in dreams or in the minds of young children, each one marvelous and distinct and alive as a new animal? This one limp and clear, like a jellyfish, that one hard and mean and secretive, like a horned snail. They could be austere and comical as top hats, or smooth and lively and flattering as ribbons. A parade of private visitors, not over yet.

"Spelling," *Who Do You Think You Are?* (p. 188)

This passage captures the sense of words as *things*, specific and sensual entities. Children often see words in this way; so do writers. There is a state of mind called *synesthesia* in which certain letters, words or numbers have specific colours or sounds. The French poet Arthur Rimbaud wrote a poem called "Vowels," beginning

A black, E white, I red, U green, O blue, vowels,
I'll tell you, one day, your hidden origins.

As children we hear more acutely — children love nonsense words and rhymes and names that make weird, enchanting sounds. I remember a Democratic Party Convention in the U.S., which my parents watched avidly on television. I wasn't sure what the convention was about, but I was pleased with the sound of candidate Senator Estes Kefauver's name and kept repeating "kee-fover" over and over.

Place names, too, are fascinating in themselves and evoke many associations: Yellowknife, Mississauga, Antarctica, Jakarta. Sometimes children make up rhymes about places, even using taboo words intended to shock the grownups. Used in these rhyming combinations, the words become more intriguing *and* more dangerous. Alice Munro, for example, gives us this rhyme in her story "Royal Beatings":

Two Vancouvers fried in snot!
Two pickled arseholes tied in a knot!
— *Who Do You Think You Are?* (p. 12)

Young Rose and her brother egg each other on to say the rhyme to their stepmother. Rose pictures the mysterious Vancouver

LANGUAGE

like an octopus in a frying pan.

Skipping-rope and clapping rhymes often involve wordplay, sometimes simply for the sound, sometimes because they flirt with forbidden words:

> Miss Molly had a steamboat
> The steamboat had a bell
> When Molly went to heaven
> The steamboat went to
> Hell-o operator ...

Hearing how words sound and developing our ear for language is very important to us as writers.

While people agree on the broad definitions of words, we also have our own personal and emotional associations to them. Diane Schoemperlen developed an entire novel from a word association test. For *In the Language of Love*, she took one hundred words used on the Kent-Rosanoff Word-Association Test and turned them into a story. Each word becomes a chapter title — e.g., Red, Table, Lake — and Schoemperlen shows the protagonist's associations with the words at different times in her life. Gradually, all the words and associations work together to tell the story, shaped by the writer's mind and craft. Some people like to make word clusters before writing about a given subject, listing all the words, ideas and feelings that come to mind about that topic.

Although humans have inborn linguistic ability, children need a sense of basic trust in the world and in the people around them in order to develop language appropriately. Loving interactions, verbal and physical, from infancy onward help build this trust. There is a story, perhaps apocryphal, that Frederick the Great of Prussia wanted to see which language children would speak if left completely on their own, hearing no language at all. Perhaps Hebrew, he thought. He hired nurses to feed and care for a group of babies, but not to talk or sing to them. However, Frederick never found out what language they would speak — they all died before their first birthday.

Although most children don't suffer this extreme fate, one of the devastating aspects of abuse is that words and statements that sound clear and simple, such as "I love you" or "This won't hurt," are misused by adults, so that trust and expectation break down. Sometimes words become weapons intended to hurt, not to communicate. I remember the childhood saying,

> Sticks and stones may break my bones
> But names will never hurt me.

This saying was probably intended to support children who were being teased, but names and other insulting words *do* hurt.

On the other hand, there are pet names and terms of endearment that convey love, friendship and security. But sometimes even loving words become hard to say if we have been hurt or rejected too often. As we will see in the chapter "Emotions," exploring these words in writing can make them feel safer to use.

Annie Finch writes: "Language is the medium where I feel the human past and future as most palpably present, in the roots and tips of the words that are always invisibly working their way through us all." (*A Formal Feeling Comes*, p. 70)

Detail and Imagery

Writing teachers often advise their students to "show, not tell." Using specific detail and interesting images helps you to create a fuller, richer word picture. *Details* let us look at things closely, clearly and intimately, using all our senses — sight, hearing, smell, touch and taste. Architect Mies van der Rohe said that "God is in the details." Part of the joy of writing is discovering more about the nature of things and people. Is the tree in your yard — or the one you see in your mind — an apple or a spruce? Knowing that will not only help you describe it better, but will tell a lot about the life and history of the tree. In the same way, rather than saying, "We ate dinner," describe the

LANGUAGE

food; talk about specific fabrics, or flowers, or the contents of your purse. The details will help you, as a writer, find the heart of your experience. Later, if you share the work with others, these specific details will help readers relate to your work.

While details describe the thing itself, *imagery* compares one thing to something else and brings your writing to life in a unique way. An image can be a *simile*, using like or as ("as cool as a cucumber," "my love is like a red, red, rose") or a *metaphor*, in which one thing seems to become another ("her heart is ice"). Although we often associate imagery with poetry, we also use it in prose, both fiction and non-fiction, and in everyday speech ("I was up the creek without a paddle").

Some images are used so frequently they become clichés (e.g., as quiet as a mouse). Try to make your images original and personal, while still connecting to your subject. The two sides of the comparison resonate with each other, so saying a dress is "as red as blood," for example, gives a different feeling than "as red as wild strawberries in June."

Imagery is often used to show emotions. A short commentary on the radio program *This Morning: The Sunday Edition* caught my attention with a powerful image. A Vancouver woman, Anna Nobile, began her story by saying, "In my family solar system, I am Pluto." We know about the solar system, and we may have heard about family systems. By combining the two in this image of Pluto — deadly cold, furthest planet from the sun — the speaker concisely presents her situation, without labelling her feelings. Taking a few moments to find a meaningful image for your situation can help you see it more clearly and write it more powerfully. As you read or hear people talk, listen for images and figures of speech, and note the ones that impress you.

Sound

Sound, too, is an important element of writing. This includes rhythm, rhyme, long or short sentences and the sounds of words and letters themselves. Say "Rat-a-tat-tat" and "Languorous lily pads" aloud, and listen to the difference.

Reading your work aloud to yourself is a good way to find your own voice; it will also reveal any false or flat notes or awkward expressions. You'll hear how the sound of the words adds richness and colour to the meaning. Often the piece makes more sense when you hear it. Reading aloud used to be a common activity for adults as well as children, and many people still do read aloud to each other, or listen to books on tape during long car trips. Writers often give readings of their work so people can hear the words aloud. A public reading is a shared group experience, like theatre, and so gives an extra dimension to the work.

Form

There are several excellent books that deal with writing in specific forms, especially in poetry. Modern poetry tends to be less formal but still uses imagery, sound and rhythm. I think of poetic language as frozen juice concentrate (before you add water), and a friend calls poetry "special effects in language." Although I will not discuss form in detail, I would like to suggest a few poetic forms that you can use working with this book.

The *list poem* is, as its name suggests, a list using interesting words or expressions. Julia Alvarez's poem "Naming the Fabrics" lists the various materials that her mother used to make clothes, paying tribute in words to what her mother created with fabric. The lists can be names of things, places or people, or responses to a situation, such as "when I can't sleep," "when I fall in love ..." Another type of list poem is the instruction poem: how to change a bicycle tire, bake bread, light a fire. In writing these instructions, step by step, you often find that a theme or meaning underlies the actions. Henry Reed's poem "Lessons of War: The Naming of Parts" is, on the surface, about military weapons instruction, but his theme makes a strong anti-war statement.

LANGUAGE

The *haiku* is a short Japanese poetic form which has found its way into English. As often taught in school, it has three lines with a total of seventeen syllables, five syllables in lines 1 and 3, and seven in line 2. Modern haiku are less rigid in form. The poems are usually drawn from nature, but may be set anywhere. They seem deceptively simple to write, but the main idea of the haiku is not just description, but depiction of a significant moment, a turning point, usually revealed in the last line. I have used haiku about the four seasons in the title pages for East, South, West and North, as each direction corresponds to one of the seasons. Here is a seventeenth-century Japanese haiku, by Basho, the poet who helped create this form:

It is so quiet
The cicada's voice
Penetrates
The rocks.

The *bantu* is an African poem of two lines, usually improvised by two people working together. One person thinks of a line, usually something she notices around her, and her partner thinks of a line in response. You can do this yourself by writing one line and free-associating to find another image suggested by your first line. You might look out the window and write:

Fresh snow on the street,

then add:

Icing on a cake.

We will look again at form in "Emotions," as some writers like to use a definite form to contain strong feelings.

Prose, although looser in form, also has certain structures. Stories have a beginning, a middle and an end. Sometimes this form is linear, progressing from start to finish, and sometimes it is circular, taking us back and forth in time and space. The characters may be tightly connected in a plot, or the story may have loose groupings of characters who weave in and out of each other's lives. Conflict and resolution has become the standard way of looking at plot, but writer and critic Janet Burroway views stories as a process of birth, "moving toward the light." This metaphor opens up new possibilities. The story need not focus on winners and losers, good and bad, but can ripple outward, or follow an ascending spiral. Perhaps stories of both kinds have their place in the world.

Style and Tone

These are elements of writing that are partly conscious, partly intuitive. They reflect your own distinctive voice. Style is the way you use language. Your style can be flowery or terse; you can use short sentences or long complex ones. You can choose colloquial or more formal language. Sometimes style changes with the kind of writing you are doing: a school report may require a different style than a letter to your mother. But often, your own personality comes through in both pieces. Style is not something we can use or not, like makeup; it is what happens every time we put pen to paper, or tell a story out loud. As an exercise or learning experience, you can try writing in a style that is very different to your usual one, just to see what that feels like. In fiction and drama, various characters each have their own style of dialogue; it is the writer's job to show this clearly.

Style and content together create the tone, or mood, of a piece of writing. The tone of a piece may be ironic, sarcastic, gently humourous, wistful, angry, reflective or objective. You might use a humourous tone to talk about serious subjects; many people agree that the best comedy comes out of pain and compassion. A friend of mine wrote several pieces about her treatment for a physical illness, and managed to find something incongruous, even funny, in each experience. She conveyed this through her language (for example, giving nicknames to the doctors, adding snippets of dialogue), and ended each sketch with the words "Things are looking up." This style and tone probably helped her make better sense of her situation and

LANGUAGE

revealed her optimistic spirit.

For beginning writers, the best advice is not to think too hard about style and tone. In fact, the more you write, the more you will develop your own style. As you revise a piece, you can think about making your language as clear as possible, not using unnecessary or "high-faluting" words and phrases. Notice how you say things, even in simple memos. I recently wrote a note to a friend saying that "Thursday would be a good day to meet," then changed it to "Thursday is a good day to meet," a more straightforward statement. Writing has its own energy; trust this energy and you will find your writing voice.

Words and Culture

An often cited observation is that the Inuit have many different words for snow. Certain words in one language and culture cannot be directly translated into the words of another. For example, in Hindi, the greeting *namaste* means "I bow down to the Supreme being in you and I recognize that you and I are one." It is used when meeting someone and when parting. Many languages have words for familial relationships that do not exist in English. In Yiddish, *machatoonim* means the relationship between the respective parents of a couple — that is, between the in-laws — a relationship that English does not recognize with a name.

Although the use of English is spreading rapidly, it is important to keep language alive in all its richness and multiplicity. If you know more than one language, or if you come from a culture that speaks another language, note in your journal some of the words and expressions that cannot be directly translated into English. Think about ways that you could use this knowledge in your writing. Perhaps you could write a piece using both languages, or a dialogue in which the speakers from different cultures have a hard time understanding each other. You could also write a meditation about how the differences in language reveal differences in attitudes and approaches to life.

This is a particularly sensitive issue for First Nations

people who attended residential schools where they were forbidden to speak their own languages, and punished for doing so. On many reserves, and in some urban schools, these languages are now being taught both to children and to adults in order to revive and claim their culture and spirituality. If your grandparents, parents or other relatives went to one of these schools, you might want to write about the way it has affected you, your family and your community.

Language and Gender

> O Canada, our home and native land
> True patriot love
> In all thy *sons* command ...

How do Canadian girls and women feel about these lines that seem to exclude them from the love of their country? I used to embarrass my son at Blue Jays' games by softly singing "... in all of *us* command," to make it gender inclusive.

Gender permeates our language. Until the last generation or two, it was common to speak of "mankind" or of "Man and his World." "Man" can be viewed as a generic word for human being, but this usage leaves the impression that the normal state of a human being is to be male.

Few people accept any more that the generic pronoun for a human being should be "he" (as in "the writer must study his craft"), but there is no simple, accepted substitute. The pronouns s/he and his/hers are awkward; he and she, her and his become tedious on repetition; common speech has long used "they" for an unknown singular subject, but the usage is generally not accepted for formal writing. I remember how, on a canoe trip with a group of women, the call "Hey, you guys, lunch is ready" sparked an hour's heated discussion over whether it was appropriate to call women "guys."

The changes in the way we speak and write reflect changes in the ways we think about gender. With changing social norms

LANGUAGE

and modern medical technology, Freud's dictum that "biology is destiny" no longer carries much conviction. We are now questioning what it means to be a man or a woman, especially in a culture like ours in which more and more opportunities are available to people of both genders, and in which it is even possible to change gender. What is the essence of femaleness or maleness?

Some people see female and male as opposites. Some believe that women have a male side, or male energy, and men have a female side. Jung calls these the "animus" and "anima" respectively. Used metaphorically, these terms apply to dynamic and receptive forces, letting go or taking in, being active or passive, being nurturing and emotional or being rational and logical. The Chinese yin-yang symbol expresses this ever-changing balance, with the dualities contained and unified in a circular pattern, each emerging from the other.

Other theorists think that masculine and feminine are not opposites but two separate dimensions, and that a person can have an abundance of both characteristics and can be simultaneously very "masculine" (assertive, forceful) and very "feminine" (gentle, nurturing). We may then ask, why call these qualities masculine and feminine at all? Why not respect each of us as an individual with various characteristics — including assertiveness, tenderness, rationality, passion — which we can use in appropriate circumstances?

Being a fiction writer, Ursula LeGuin did not propound a theory on the effect of gender. Instead, she envisioned a new world and populated it with people who are born neither male nor female. In her novel *The Left Hand of Darkness*, people have no gender until they come into monthly heat, or *kemmer*. At that time, they find someone else also in *kemmer*, and through various hormonal changes, one of the pair becomes male and one female. If conception occurs, the pregnant person remains female long enough to bear and nurse the child; otherwise, they both return to their previous state, and during the next *kemmer* may take on the other gender. This world has no masculinity or femininity; no men's work and women's work; and no male and female pronouns. There are conflicts, but no war and no rape. This shows the power of fiction: it helps us rethink our own world and the dualities we take for granted.

Do men and women speak different languages? In *You Just Don't Understand: Women and Men in Conversation*, linguistics professor Deborah Tannen argues that women and men have different, but equally valid, conversational styles. Men often seek to establish vertical hierarchies, while women tend to prefer horizontal networks and connections and share stories of their lives and everyday experiences, sometimes derided as "gossip." Men are more likely to respond to a friend's problem by offering practical suggestions, while women are more apt to respond with empathy and rapport. Men's style, however, has been regarded as the normative, so it is often women who are told to change or adapt.

Gender, however, is not the only influence on language; our cultures and our personalities also play a large role. You need not try to imitate "men's" style of writing, but neither need you feel constrained to write "like a woman." Find your own voice and write as yourself. Likewise, I believe that anyone can read anything and use it as appropriate for her own expression. Women should read and support other women's writing, but we need not cut ourselves off from the centuries of literary history: Homer, Shakespeare, Dickens, Li Po and Basho are part of our heritage. As Adele Wiseman writes in her *Memoirs*, writing "is, after all, an ongoing expression of our common humanity."(p. 59)

A related question is whether women can write about men's experience, and vice versa. I believe they can, although it may be harder to imagine the "other," and we may need to research some of the details of another person's life — even something as mundane as shaving. Lucy Maud Montgomery's character, *Emily of New Moon*, wrote a sketch of her teacher in which she knew, somehow, that "he wore a black coat on certain days so he wouldn't feel so drunk." How did she know? This is an example of the writing mind that can get inside someone else's skin and report back.

What Was That Word Again?

As you go along, you will want to acquire some tools of the trade. You don't have to rush out and get any or all of these right away, and you can certainly start writing without them. You can keep in your journal a list of new and interesting words that you discover. As you get hooked, you may want to find a good dictionary, and perhaps also a rhyming dictionary and an etymological dictionary (dealing with word origins); a thesaurus (synonyms and antonyms); an atlas; books that might help with particular subjects or imagery, such as mythology, history, gardening, animal books, cookbooks, Bartlett's quotations, a book of names.

It is also helpful to have a book on writing style, such as Strunk and White's *Elements of Style* or *The Chicago Manual of Style*. There are also many excellent books about the writing process, which can inspire you, build up your confidence and suggest further exercises and ways of writing. You will find a selection of these in the bibliography, and discover others by browsing in your local bookstore or library. Keep near you a few assorted books that you really enjoy. Find quotes, pictures and cartoons to put by your desk or to tape inside your journal.

Finally, as Adrienne Rich emphasizes in *What is Found There: Notebooks on Poetry and Politics,* language is not only the way we say things, but the transformative power of imagination itself. We need to use the language we inherit, and continually re-create it to make it work meaningfully in our own lives.

EXERCISES

1. *People-Startling Words*

Write a list of a dozen words that are startling or interesting — words you love, words you hate, words that make you uncomfortable, words whose sounds are lovely even if you don't know the meaning. Then use several together in a paragraph or brief story. You might want to give your list a theme — words from sports, animal names, or a subject you like — or you might want to choose a wide range of words.

If you are in a writing group, you can do this exercise together, finding ways to share your words. One way is to pass a paper around the circle, collecting one word from each member of the group. Each person then uses that list of words to write a paragraph or a poem.

A variation is for each person to write down five words or images she uses often, and then exchange papers; each of you then write a short piece using another person's words.

2. *Mix and Match*
(Adapted from *Writing Down the Bones*, by Natalie Goldberg)

Write a list of ten nouns (e.g., baby, dragon, stars). Then a list of ten verbs (e.g., fly, cry, die). Number your lists. Then write sentences matching noun #1 to verb #1, and so on. They might sound wildly mismatched, but sometimes in this odd juxtaposition, interesting and meaningful images arise. For example, "stars" and "cry." Stars don't cry, you think. But what about: "The stars look down on earth and cry over spilt blood." This ability to play with words, to try out new combinations, can help us break free from ordinary ways of looking at the world. Bypassing our logical mind, we come up with some new truths. Some of your sentences will work better than others. And you may find a sentence or two that will lead to a longer piece of writing.

LANGUAGE

3. *He, She, or It*

This is the title of a novel by the American novelist and poet Marge Piercy. For this exercise, write a short story or dialogue, with two or three characters, in which the gender of at least one of the characters is not apparent. (One way to avoid the pronoun problem could be to write in the first person "I," or in the second person, "you.") Jeanette Winterson did this in her novel *Written on the Body*, a love triangle in which there is a married couple, man and woman, and a narrator who loves the woman and whose gender is deliberately not defined.

4. *Images*

Think of six clichés (e.g., "as hungry as a horse") and find a fresher, more original way to express that idea.

*

Who Am I?

Somewhere a rose opens
And its scent is you.
— Eva Tihanyi, "Somewhere"

WE BECOME WHO WE ARE through birth and heritage, temperament, talents, choices, experiences and accidents, lucky or unlucky. Thus, though some things do not change about ourselves, other things are always changing, adding to the roles that we take on throughout our lives. In the film *Fiction and Other Truths*, novelist Jane Rule says:

> Each of us is made up of a number of minorities, some of them privileged, some of them problematic. I am white, I am well-educated and I am well-off. Those privileges could teach me to be smug, judgemental and condescending, or they could teach me to take responsibility for the gifts I have and compassion for those who had not been so blessed. I am also a woman, a lesbian and an arthritic. Any of these could have taught me to be a bitter victim. I hope they have taught me instead courage and humour.

She adds that we need to integrate these different parts of ourselves so that we can "go into the world and do (our) work with joy."

There is always an interplay between ourselves as unique individuals and as members of various groups. It is important to be aware of how these groups affect us, and how we affect them. For example, in her book *Shaking the Rattle: Healing the Trauma of Colonization*, Barbara-Helen Hill reminds her readers that what they do and how they act will affect the next seven generations.

Hill also notes the traumatic effects on many First Nations people of being treated *only* as a group. If we are seen only as a member of a certain group (e.g., lesbian, Native, Black, Jewish, Oriental, people on welfare, disabled, elderly, alcoholics, women), our individual identity is invalidated, especially when these groups are oppressed or demeaned by those in power. We may begin to see ourselves that way as well and perhaps internalize some of the hatred shown towards us. (Hill calls this experience "ethnostress.") On the other hand, it is important to be responsible to people in the various groups and communities in which we find ourselves or with which we interact. These groups can also help us establish our identity.

The exercises in this book may serve as mirrors showing different parts of yourself, parts you had forgotten or do not recognize. This may be a bit scary at first. However, these are not distorting fun-house mirrors, but ones which, I hope, will reveal more aspects of your wholeness. As Morgan, a Hamilton poet, wrote about seeing her reflection,

> I looked at the stranger in the mirror and asked,
> "Where have we met before?"

You can do the exercises more than once, at different times in your life or in different voices. As writers, even beginning writers, we move back and forth between our own identities and those of others; we use our imagination and our empathy to discover and know the life of the world as well as our own personal lives. This is part of the role of the writer and other artists, as Jane Rule emphasizes:

> Every artist seems to me to have the job to bear witness to the world we live in. To some extent, I think of all of us as artists because we have voices and we are each of us unique, and so if we don't bear witness, as citizens, as people, as individuals, the right that we

East

have had to life is sacrificed. There is a silence instead of a speaking presence.

— *Fictions and Other Truths*

Exercises

1. *Minorities*

Write down four groups/categories to which you belong, or have belonged, and write a few lines about how each has affected you, now or in the past. These can include culture, geographic origin, physical attributes, career, education, economic situation, sexual orientation and family status (e.g., mother or daughter, married or divorced).

2. *If I Were ...*
(Adapted from *Poem Crazy: Freeing your Life with Words*, by Susan Goldsmith Wooldridge)

This exercise may sound a bit childish or dreamlike, but it can help you discover some things about yourself and can also be a lot of fun. It might be interesting to do this now, and again after you have worked on the exercises in this book and done more of your own writing. This is also a good exercise to do with a writing friend or in a group. The exercise has several steps, which are important to follow in order.

1) Write down the answers to these questions, noting the first thing that comes to mind:

    If I were a colour, what colour would I be?
    What shape?
    What movement?
    What sound?
    What animal?

WHO AM I?

What song?
What food?
What number?
What car, or other vehicle?
What piece of furniture?
What food?
What musical instrument?
What place?
What element in nature (e.g., planet, ocean)?
What kind of tree?
What is something I'm afraid of?
What is the word hiding behind my eyes?

2) After you have written the answers to these questions, combine two or three or more into sentences beginning with "I am," adding action and descriptive words as necessary to link them together: e.g., "I am a turquoise unicorn spinning in a tornado," "I am French toast singing the blues on a rainy Sunday morning."

3) Now see if you can put these sentences together into a poem. You can repeat "I am" several times to create a pattern, or vary it with "I will be," "I want to be," and so on. You may want to omit some of the answers or think of other questions.

Children can be good at doing this exercise, because their imaginations are a bit more playful. So, if you are having trouble getting started, think of how you might have answered the questions when you were three, or six, or ten.

Here is a poem written by a girl of fourteen with learning and emotional problems, who lives in a foster home.

> I am
> soft as a kitten
> that loves to eat ice-cream
> I am
> a pink heart

driving a Honda Accord
on a very sunny day
I am
afraid of electricity
I am
in love with Kevin
I love skating
and I am
stayin' alive
like a snail
on a two-person love-seat.

These are dreamlike images that capture something about who we are at this moment.

3. Secret Names

T.S. Eliot wrote that cats have three names: the name the family uses everyday, a second more dignified and particular name and a third that is known only to the cat. If you have, or have had, a secret name for yourself, write it in your journal. Write about the person who has this special name. How is she like you, and how is she different?

4. I Used to Be, but Now I Am ...

(This exercise was developed by Kenneth Koch.) Write images that describe how you were before and how you are now. You can be literal, fanciful, humorous (I used to be an egg, but now I am scrambled; I used to be blue and red, but now I am marooned.) You can talk about your own life (I used to be young, but now I'm older), or invent a life (I used to be a belly dancer, but now I dance with wolves). One person I knew did a series of linked images: I used to be a tree, but now I'm cut down. I used to be wood, but now I'm a chair. I used to be in the living room, but now I'm in the basement.

WHO AM I?

Write a page of these images. Keep your hand moving and let go of your logical mind. Try to do some that are linked and some that are not.

❉

Beginnings

ELIZABETH BLACKWELL, the first woman to graduate from medical school in the United States, attended the only college that would take her, Geneva Medical College in upstate New York, near Lake Seneca. She graduated in 1849, one year after the Convention of Women's Rights was held in the nearby town of Seneca Falls.

A century and a half later, I was on the same campus (now Hobart-William Smith College) to attend the Feminist Women's Writing Workshops, a turning point in my becoming a writer. On campus, there is a statue of Elizabeth Blackwell with this inscription:

I congratulate myself that I have, at last, found the right place for my beginning.

This statement seems full of hope. It suggests that we can begin again and again, and have many changes of direction. Further, it suggests that we know, intuitively, when we have found the right place — or at least *a* right place — to begin an important part of our lives.

What are you hoping to begin in your life? Or what have you recently begun? A new job? A relationship with someone? A garden? Starting a journal is a beginning. If you have a large goal, like going on a vacation or going back to school, break this down into smaller more manageable steps. Elizabeth Blackwell, for example, was a teacher and studied privately with various doctors before she applied and was accepted to medical school. Even if something seems far away, there may be some things you can do here and now to make a start.

And we can *congratulate* ourselves on our beginnings; we can feel good about our decision to take the first step, and take pride in it. This is something many people, especially women, have a hard time doing.

Now think about *place*. Are you in a place that feels right for your beginning, or do you need to be in some other place? Visualize what that place would be like. What would it take to get there?

Some people use the butterfly's life cycle as a metaphor for describing a given project or enterprise: are you the egg (new beginning), the caterpillar (exploring and getting started), in the cocoon (developing your idea into reality), or the emerging butterfly (completion, and sharing your idea with the world)? Of course, this is never a final stage, because the butterfly lays more eggs, creating a new beginning. It is interesting that in Greek mythology the butterfly is a symbol of the soul.

The right place for a beginning suggests a place that is safe but not restricting, open to new possibilities and challenges. Think back to earlier beginnings in your life, such as your first day of school, your childhood home or the first place you lived on your own. What mental pictures do you have of this place? If your memories were a video, where would you want to pause, rewind, fast-forward?

Exercises

1. *The Right Place*

Describe a place where you have had a new beginning, using all five senses — sight, hearing, smell, taste, touch — as well as your emotions. You can write about the physical characteristics of the place, and include the people and activities around you.

2. No Place Like Home

Home is where we start from, and also the place we are looking for. There is a telling expression, "safe as houses." Even when the house is not safe, most people find a particular place where they feel safe and secure. Describe a room in your house (or a house you often visited) that was a safe place for you as a child. Write about the furnishings; your special belongings in the room; whom, if anyone, you shared the room with; and finally, why this was a safe place for you.

3. Congratulations

Write a paragraph, or a page, beginning with the line "I congratulate myself on ..." You may want to keep coming back to this line as you write, using it as a refrain to remind yourself of both your courage and your accomplishments.

FOOD AND CLOTHING

FOOD AND CLOTHING are basic to life and to our everyday lives. We eat almost from the time we are born until we die, and we wear some kind of clothing much of that time. These are simple, material things, but our reaction to them is far from simple. We have foods we love, foods we hate; foods we were forced to eat as children; foods we won't eat because we are dieting or can't eat for religious or medical reasons. Food can be connected with family dinners and relationships, with lovers, with strangers on our travels.

Food can be associated with memories of hunger, even starvation. Refugees, survivors of war or concentration camps, or people with personal or family memories of poverty and of droughts and other natural disasters may have very different attitudes towards food than those who have grown up with relative plenty. Farmers and rural people have different views about food than do city-dwellers. Those who work with food have still different impressions. In addition, there are definite cultural attitudes towards food in general and towards certain foods in particular.

People who have, or who have overcome, eating disorders such as anorexia and bulimia will, of course, have their own stories and emotions about food and eating. It is disturbing and ironic that food, the source of life, can become connected to illness and death. A colleague and I have been collecting fiction, poetry and creative non-fiction for a potential anthology about eating disorders, and we have been moved and surprised by the range of material. We have found that, for some people, creative writing is a first step towards healing; others can only write about the depth of the illness *after* they have started their recovery.

Food is often deeply connected to memories of childhood: favourite foods, treats, our parents' and grandparents' attitudes towards food. Did you have to eat everything on your plate at dinner, or even cold the next morning? Were there special foods you only ate on holidays, or in the homes of certain relatives or family friends? How have these traditions been carried on, or lost? I could write, for example, about my great-grandmother's jelly cakes, pastry squares filled with apple and jam, which she taught my mother to make and which I learned partly from my mother and partly on my own, baking them first in a communal kitchen in California at Christmas. Handing down recipes and cooking together are time-honoured ways for women to share their stories and experiences.

Sometimes, letting yourself enjoy a simple food, alone or with a friend, becomes a celebration of life. The first peach of summer, a perfect soft-boiled egg or an ice-cream cone at just the right moment are small miracles.

Eating, and specific dishes, often play an important part in fiction. Some novels even include recipes; not surprisingly, these are almost always by women. In *Like Water for Chocolate*, by Laura Esquivel, food becomes an element of the book's magic realism, turning emotions into concrete reality. When a jealous cook cries into the cake batter, all the wedding guests become sick. Quail with rose petals becomes an instant aphrodisiac, affecting the characters and even the landscape.

In writing, as in life, food often acts as substitute for sex. I once wrote a poem about cooking an octopus. The poem was primarily about the octopus itself and the odd, primitive experience of handling and cooking it, but it was also about an erotic encounter following the meal, and about more generalized elements of violence, sensuality and mystery in our lives.

FOOD AND CLOTHING

Clothing, too, can have erotic significance: not only Victoria's Secret lingerie, but even red wool socks worn to bed. Clothes show how we feel about ourselves, and also present an image to the world. We have everyday clothes, fancy clothes, ceremonial clothes, work clothes, new clothes, old favourites and hand-me-downs.

Most children love to dress up and, for a time, become someone completely different; this is part of the reason holidays like Halloween and Purim are so popular. Acting or dancing is another opportunity to dress up and consciously take on a different identity. It is not surprising that many plays and fairy tales involve transformation through the donning of a garment.

More subtly, however, all our changes of clothes allow us to play different parts, experiment with identities. In my heart of hearts, I love net, glitters and sequins, though I never buy or wear them. The nearest I came was a blue silky outfit with rhinestones and glitter that my son picked out for my Chanukah present when he was six. Maybe he saw through my jeans and sweaters and my earnest readings to him of *The Paper Bag Princess*, and guessed my secret. (A close second was the flowing white negligee, stained with red wine, that I wore when I acted in a Tennessee Williams play in college.)

In Henry James' *Portrait of a Lady*, worldly-wise Madame Merle says, "I know a large part of myself is in the clothes I choose to wear." The young heroine Isobel Archer, still innocent of the world, counters that her clothes, imposed on her by society, reflect the dressmaker's taste, not her own. Madame Merle replies, "Should you prefer to go without them?"

How much do you think your clothes express yourself, and how much do they conform to other people's tastes and wishes?

East

EXERCISES

1. *Family Recipes*

Write down a family recipe. Then write about where it comes from, who taught it to you, the occasions when you cook it, what it says about your family, and any other things that come to mind.

2. *Favourite Clothing*

Think of one of your favourite pieces of clothing, now or in the past. It could be a coat, a pair of shoes, a T-shirt, even a nightgown or an old sweater. Write a page or two, telling the story of this garment: where it came from, why you like it, when you wear it and how it makes you feel.

3. *Grocery Lists*

a) Write your typical grocery list, then take one of the items and write about it — why you need this item, any past associations to it, what, if anything, you might buy instead.

b) Write a grocery or shopping list with seven to ten items that you would *never* buy. Create a character who might have written this list and would really buy these products. What would she (or he) be like? Age? Marital status? Children? Where does this person live? Would you like to meet this person? Why would she need the items on the list?

4. *My First Bra*

This usually evokes vivid memories. You could begin, "I remember when I got my first bra." Or you could write about "My Last Bra," if you've stopped wearing them.

LANDSCAPE AND SENSE OF PLACE

On every side, far and near — east, west, north and south — it was all forest, a boundless sea of forest, within whose leafy recesses lay hidden as infinite a variety of life and movement as within the depths of the ocean; and it reposed in the noontide so still and so vast!

A Canadian settler hates a tree, regards it as his natural enemy, as something to be destroyed, annihilated by all and any means.

— Anna Jameson, *Winter Studies and Summer Rambles in Canada*

CANADA IS A COUNTRY OF LANDSCAPE and weather, forest and water and mountain, snow and brief summer sunshine. These two quotes by Anna Jameson show the deep split in our relationship to the land: appreciating its abundance and variety, and destroying it for profit. This was occurring even in 1837, when Jameson arrived in Upper Canada. Today, writing about nature often involves looking at the damage caused by pollution, industrial growth and other environmental hazards.

More quickly than we want to imagine, the land is disappearing and the health of the land is ebbing away. There are many losses. Habitats for ducks, frogs, butterflies. Clean water. Woodland and meadows, covered with shopping malls. Back in 1970 Joni Mitchell wrote, "They paved paradise and put in a parking lot." Things have only gotten worse since then.

In this chapter, we will look at landscape and nature, and also at the sense of place in writing, whether that is a city street or a forest path, a tenement or a tent. Places exist in time as well as space, history as well as geography, and when we let ourselves be fully aware, we can write about a place on all these levels.

Because Canada is a vast country encompassing many kinds of terrain, the land has been an important element of storytelling and writing, from Aboriginal legends onward. Native peoples believed, and still believe, in living in harmony with the land, water and air and all the creatures in it, as well as with the seasons, weather and spiritual forces. They can see the presence of spirit in all aspects of nature.

Explorers, missionaries and traders brought new ways of looking at the land. They often viewed the land and its creatures as hostile, something to be conquered, tamed or owned.

The different cultural perspective shows itself even in grammar. Richard Green, a writer who lives on the Six Nations reserve in Ohsweken, Ontario, told me that a white, English-speaking person would usually write "John paddles his canoe across the river," with the noun "John" and the verb "paddles" having the predominant place, while a speaker of one of the Iroquoian languages would say, "Across the river John paddles his canoe," the setting "across the river" being most important, John and the canoe contained within it.

In the early part of this century, literature courses in Canada looked to English and American writing. Since then, more and more writers have explored the sense of place in Canada, across the provinces. When W.O. Mitchell died in 1998, I read a tribute by a writer who said that Mitchell's early writing about the prairies, such as *Who Has Seen the Wind?*, made her realize that the place where she lived was, indeed, worth writing about.

Like the West in the United States, the North in Canada is a frontier, natural and mythic, where people go to seek their fortunes and test their limits. As Robert Service wrote, "There are strange things done in the midnight sun" ("The Cremation of Sam McGee"). Margaret Atwood used this image as the title for her book *Strange Things: The Malevolent North in Canadian*

Literature. Many people find the North haunting and beautiful, like other wild places in the world.

Indeed, the natural world is part of our sense of place. We often feel restored and refreshed by being in nature, whether it is an hour's walk on a hiking trail, a week-long canoe trip or just looking up at the stars on a clear night. In nature, we learn to be aware in a new way, to be there in the moment to see a butterfly or hear a cardinal, and to sense the vastness of time represented by mountains and sequoia trees, deserts and oceans. We can let ourselves look with "wide attention," rather than "narrow attention," in the words of Marion Milner. The narrow focus is task-oriented and logical, necessary at certain times. At other times, however, it is good to be able to shift into wide focus, attentive but not expecting anything from the situation or ourselves.

Nature is not the only kind of place about which one can write. A strong, concrete description of any place, whether it is a glittering shop, a dingy tenement, a vibrant street or an immaculate hospital, can ground a piece of writing and bring it to life.

Another aspect of place is the pull between "here" and "away." We can articulate the distances between leaving home and going somewhere else, whether from one province to another, or from another part of the world to settle in Canada. We can write of both nostalgia and discovery.

Except for the Aboriginal people who came to this land thousands of years ago, Canada is a nation of immigrants, some more recent than others. More and more, people come from many far-flung places, adding to the mosaic of cultures. Many immigrants cannot, or do not want to, go home, for political or personal reasons. If this is your case, you can remember your homeland through writing and also record the strangeness of a new land. Writing stories for children is often a good way to deal with these feelings of newness, strangeness, being "lost and found," and a way to reclaim places and traditions.

East

Places seen in childhood have a particular fix on the mind and emotions. The sensuous details are important: What did the grass or the dirt feel like? What smells were in the air? What scared you, or made you feel peaceful? What were the holidays like? You can use this in your writing, whether you still live in the place where you grew up or a place thousands of kilometres away.

Landscapes can exist in the imagination as well as in the physical world, as in science fiction and fantasy (e.g., the rivers, stark mountains, golden forests and grim plains of J.R.R. Tolkien's *Lord of the Rings*). Fantastic places need details as vivid and specific as factual ones to give the place an ongoing life and the characters a coherent world to inhabit.

In addition, landscapes can be internal as well as external. Marilyn Gear Pilling, a Hamilton poet, explores inner landscapes in *The Field Next to Love*. This field is one of the landmarks in her inner world:

> ... and in me, familiar occupies the field
> next to love; there are places along the border
> where I cannot tell one from the other.

Exercises

1. *Talking to the Wind*

Have a dialogue with something in nature that you remember from childhood or that you see in your life now. As a child in New York, I could play in Central Park, and I remember spending hours ensconced in my "tree house," a niche in a white birch tree where the main trunk split into four large branches. Write what you say, and also what the object or force in nature says. (An example of this is Frank O'Hara's poem, "A True Account of Talking to the Sun at Fire Island," which was

LANDSCAPE AND SENSE OF PLACE

his take on Vladimir Mayakovsky's "An Amazing Adventure," in which Mayakovsky also talks to the sun.)

2. *In the Picture*

Find a painting or photograph of a place/scene that intrigues you. It could be the country, a town, the city or the seashore. It could even be an abstract painting that suggests a place. One young woman in a writing group described a modern Cubist picture that reminded her of a stray cat in an alley at night. Perhaps there are people in the picture, perhaps not. Write about what you see in this picture, what you imagine has just happened, is happening, will happen next. Are you in the picture, are you watching from outside, or are you looking at it from another time? Try to experience and describe the details, using all your senses. Find the story, the energy, the secret in the picture.

3. *Inner Landscapes*

Landscapes can describe different emotions or states of being. What kind of landscape would jealousy have? What would love's landscape be like? Choose at least four different emotions to describe in this way and write a paragraph for each one. You can use landscapes you have seen, or try to imagine them. A variation of this exercise is to describe the landscape of your own inner world, a place where you go to retreat, to explore or to discover yourself.

4. *Haibun: Journalling and Haiku*

Haibun (pronounced "high-bun") is a Japanese form of journalling, with interspersed haiku poems to highlight certain things. Becky Alexander, a poet from Cambridge, Ontario, has written a book in this form, *On Raven's Wings*. Journalling allows the writer to be discursive, to let her thoughts ramble. In the haiku, she distills this experience into one or two images. Here

East

is an example from Becky's book, an account of a three-day retreat:

> I awake to bird song and the dawn.
> It is too early, no work today. One
> slow movement, I roll back to sleep.
>
> *The silver slice of dawn*
> *wedges itself*
> *between dark and light.*

Find a place you can be alone and wander, or sit and observe. Write a paragraph or two in your journal, then write a haiku that is another view of the experience. As you look through your journal notes, you may only have to select and rearrange a few words to create this small poem, which feels as though it can be held in your hand like a smooth stone.

You may want to refer back to the subsection on "Form" in the "Language" chapter, to refresh your memory of how to write a haiku.

❖

South

Summer
Fire
Physical vitality
the Child within ... Play, Trust,
Making Relationships

Crescent moon
Sliver of orange magic
On a summer night.

— Gina Shelton
"Seasons"

Talking to Your Body

I AM A WIDE WOMAN
Broad. Broader. Broaden your view
Take me in as I am — full view.
— Mary Billy, "Taking Notice,"
We'Moon '00 Calendar

WE ALL ARE BORN into a body. It can be the source of great joys and ordinary pleasures — nursing as a baby, making love, running hard, smelling a rose, swimming in the ocean, warming up beside a campfire or under blankets on a cold night, giving birth, nursing and holding a baby — whatever takes your fancy. But it can also be the source of our greatest terrors — torture, abuse, rape, starvation, painful illness, crippling accidents. In addition, our bodies are sometimes awkward, embarrassing, unable to meet our expectations. Still, they are ours, as long as we keep breathing.

Throughout this book, I talk about the interconnection of mind and body. Even if our bodies become hurt or ill, we still live in and through that body. Even the life of the mind and imagination comes to us in physical, sensory ways, *as if* we were living the experience in our body.

Most babies and young children love themselves, including their bodies, totally and completely: their toes, their elbows, their fingers. When a baby takes the nipple of a breast or bottle in her mouth, she enjoys the food and tactile sensation and also

South

begins to learn about her world. Watching young children move and play, we often see how they feel at home in their bodies. But as we move through the school years and into adolescence, comparisons and doubts about ourselves, including our physical selves, begin to usurp that early self-confidence. Sometimes it takes quite a while to regain it.

I remember a picture-book I had as a child, *My Mother is the Most Beautiful Woman in the World*, by Becky Reyher. Set in nineteenth-century Russia, the book shows a small girl falling asleep in the wheat fields while her parents are harvesting. She wakes up, lost and alone, and is found by people from a strange village who ask about her parents. "My mother is the most beautiful woman in the world," she says. The villagers send out word and all the known beauties of nearby communities come rushing to see if this is their child. The little girl keeps saying "No, that's not my mother." Finally, a woman described as heavy-set, missing several teeth, with blotchy skin, misshapen nose and stringy hair comes along, breathing heavily from running. The little girl runs up, embraces her and says, "See, I told you my mother is the most beautiful woman in the world."

I identified with this book in a special way, since my Russian great-grandmother, whom I knew and loved, resembled the mother in the story. I had already learned from her that beauty is more than skin-deep. My great-grandmother, unlike her daughter and her daughter's daughter, existed simply and comfortably in her own (ample) skin, without trying to create a particular look or fit into anyone else's concept of beauty.

Many of us may remember the way our grandmothers and great-grandmothers accepted the reality of their own bodies. What happened, then, to their daughters and daughters' daughters (like my grandmother and mother, like myself at times in my life)? What makes women come to criticize and dislike their bodies and pass on this discomfort to their own daughters? In striving to meet a standard of perfect beauty to which their own inherited facial features and bodily type do not conform, they objectify and try to tame the body instead of listening to it.

In some people, this goes to extremes, just as some people try to control nature, the body of Mother Earth, more stringently than do others. For instance, I have a friend who, since adolescence, has spent painful hours having electrolysis to her legs and face, and silently measures her food as she eats. And although my friend's actions trouble me, and as a teenager made me question my own body, I can see how much she was conditioned by family, culture and personal experiences. Women often say that "men want us to look this way," and certainly the media and the "beauty" and fashion industries try to convince us that each new trend will make us more desirable. We internalize all these messages about our bodies, along with the ridicule and teasing so common in childhood.

Negative feelings can also come from not seeing our own bodies reflected in magazines, films or television programs. Women of colour and women who have physical and mental challenges have, until recently, hardly seen themselves at all. This invisibility can send the message that they must be less desirable.

We must remember that standards of beauty vary throughout the world and throughout history. In Renaissance Europe and in many non-Caucasian societies today, women we might call fat were, and are, considered beautiful. By today's standards, Marilyn Monroe would be considered overweight. The thin-to-the-point-of-starvation look for models and actresses may be contributing to the increase of anorexia nervosa among young women and makes a mockery of real starvation in other parts of the world.

When we feel good about our body, we can listen to what it needs for good health and pleasure, without hurting or overdisciplining ourselves

In a recent book, *You're So Fat: Exploring Ojibway Discourse*, Roger Sprelman notes that when he and his wife were living in

South

an Ojibway community in northern Ontario, she left briefly to attend her father's funeral. When she returned a few weeks later, people told her "You're so fat!" as a compliment, meaning that she hadn't pined away from grief. Having enough food to survive lean times was essential to this community, so being "fat" was a virtue rather than a defect. Unfortunately, she (a non-Native person, like her husband) went on a diet shortly after these comments.

Barbara Crooker of Pennsylvania has written a poem called "Starving for the Gold," about an imaginary Olympic gymnast's struggle with anorexia. The poem was triggered by her daughter's recovery from this disorder, and by her compassion for many women athletes, including Christy Henrich, elite gymnast, who said: "It feels like there's a beast inside me, a monster. It feels evil." The poem ends with the young woman finding the body image that she craves:

> Her mind had hooked itself to perfection's fish:
> a body with no disfiguring fat,
> lighter than the Russians,
> lighter than air.
> She wanted to be a swan.
> She wanted to have elastic bands for bones,
> no nerves,
> a body light and fluid
> as a pink satin ribbon
> floating in the wind.
> She wanted to let go
> the bounds of earth.
> And did.

It is not only in our times that women's bodies have been moulded and distorted. Consider Victorian corsets and the binding of women's feet in China, still within recent memory.

In a clear, compassionate and groundbreaking book, *Lost Voices: Women, Chronic Pain, and Abuse,* family physician Nellie A.

Radomsky links women's symptoms of chronic pain, often hard to treat medically, to their stories of past and present abuse and stress. She says that women and men both suffer chronic pain, but women more often have pain where no direct biological problem can be identified. In a biomedical model, these women usually face two alternatives: either they are given a series of tests, confusing and exhausting for patient and doctor, or they are dismissed with the comment "it's all in your head," leaving them feeling unheard, unbelieved, even crazy. When Dr. Radomsky began listening to the life stories of the women in her office, she became more aware of the subtle and not-fully-understood ways that abuse and emotional stress affect the body, and the ways that long-term changes in attitude, life-style and self-care affect recovery. This is not by any means to say that all illness results from something amiss in our lives, a position dangerously close to blaming the victim of disease.

A recent anthology, *Women's Bodies/Women's Lives: Health, Well-Being and Body Image* (edited by Miedema, Stoppard and Anderson) has for its central premise the "belief that women's bodies and women's lives are inseparable — each can be understood only within the context of the other." So, the more women see themselves as subjects and participants, not objects or patients, the more they can feel in control of both their bodies and their lives. In addition, the authors of the various essays question the prevailing dualistic view that mind and body are separate things. An alternative view sees mind and body as closely interconnected, together creating a whole person.

People who do breath-work and body-work (e.g., yoga, Tai-Chi, dance) find that "each thought is felt and experienced in our bodies," as Barbara Lynn Cull-Wilby says in her essay "Breath and Body Wisdom" (*Women's Bodies/Women's Lives*). She adds that "Our bodies talk not only through voice and thoughts and language but also through an infinite array of expressions: mobility, posture, breathing depth, sight, smell, touch, to name a few." Body work sometimes releases old tensions, feelings and memories and stimulates new insights, which can help you in your writing and your everyday life. In addition, we usually feel better, emotionally as well as physically, when we move and use our bodies as well as we can.

In *Angels of Flesh, Angels of Silence,* Lorna Crozier has written wonderful poems about the body, including several about women with breast cancer. "Nothing Missing" deals with a friend who has lost a breast to cancer. Hearing of another woman who has filled her empty bra cup with birdseed, the two women imagine the results of such a breast:

> And what of sprouting?
> Green tendrils
> Crawling up her cleavage.
>
> I imagine Mary sitting in a park
> surrounded by sparrows and chickadees,
> the brave ones lighting
> on her hair, her arms,
> her soft, full breasts.

Another of Crozier's poems, "Without Hands," is "in memory of Victor Jara, the Chilean musician whose hands were smashed by the military, to prevent him from playing his guitar and singing for his fellow prisoners in the Santiago stadium. Along with thousands of others, he was tortured and finally killed there in September, 1973." Without mentioning this violence, the poem simply and beautifully invokes personal, domestic, and natural images of what our lives would be like, missing our hands.

> WITHOUT HANDS
>
> All the machines in the world
> stop. The textile machines, the paper machines,
> the machines in the mines turning stones to fire.
> Without hands to touch them, spoons, forks and knives

TALKING TO YOUR BODY

forget their names and uses, the baby is not bathed,
bread rises on the stove, overflows the bowl.
Without hands, the looms
stop. The music
    stops.
The plums turn sweet and sticky and gather flies.

Without hands
    without those beautiful conjunctions
those translators of skin, bone, hair
two eyes go blind
two pale hounds sniffing ahead and doubling back
to tell us
    of hot and cold or the silk of roses after rain
are lost
    two terns feeling the air in every feather
are shot down.

Without hands my father doesn't plant potatoes
row on row, build a house for wrens,
or carry me
from the car to bed
when I pretend I'm sleeping.
On wash-days my mother doesn't hang clothes
on the line, she doesn't turn the pages of a book
and read out loud,
or teach me how to lace my shoes.

Without hands my small grandmother
doesn't pluck the chicken for our Sunday meal
or every evening, before she goes to sleep,
brush and brush her long white hair.

   The "without" theme can also be used in writing about other things: "Without Cats," "Without Trees," "Without Names." This last reminds me of Ursula LeGuin's short story "She Unnames Them" (*Buffalo Gals and Other Animal Presences*) which is about Eve un-naming the animals, returning to a state of being before Adam's categorizing.

EXERCISES

1. *Body Language*

One way of getting to know your own body is to write *as if a part of your body is speaking*: perhaps your hands, your hair, your eyes, your breasts, your feet. It can even be a part of the body that is missing (either from birth or because of surgery, illness or accident).

Do a timed writing of fifteen minutes. Before you start writing, take three deep breaths, relax your body in a way that feels comfortable to you and see if you can hear the voice of a particular body part. It may be something you and others can see (hair, feet, breasts), or an organ deep inside. It may be an area where you have been experiencing illness or pain. You might try writing several pieces about different areas of your body, including parts you like as well as those you don't like or those that are causing you concern.

The writing can be a series of paragraphs, a poem, a letter from your body part to you, or a dialogue between the two of you.

2. *I'm a Beauty*

Laura Smith is a singer from Nova Scotia. Her song, "I'm a Beauty" (on her CD *it's a personal thing*) is about loving and accepting your body as the key to loving yourself. In the song, she sings to various parts of her body (her hands, her eyes) and encourages us to "look deep" because the deeper we look, the greater the surprise at observing our own beauty.

Let yourself believe you are truly a beauty. Write a piece called "I'm Beautiful Because ..."

3. Facing a Challenge

Write about a time when you took on a challenging physical experience, anything from climbing a mountain to walking on crutches after an accident. Describe the event with as much detail as you can. How did this experience affect your feelings about your body?

4. "Liar, Liar!"

This exercise can lead to writing that is more like a poem or story than a journal entry. It embodies the idea of "lies that tell the truth." Make up a lie about your body, or a part of your body, and write about it. You might imagine you are very tall or very small (like Alice in Wonderland), or that parts of your body can grow back, like the lizard's tail, or that you do have "eyes in the back of your head" (as your mother said *she* did), or that you can turn into a tree or become invisible at will. I myself, at a height of exactly five feet (well, maybe a fraction less) might write about being *The Biggest Modern Woman of the World*, as in the title of one of Susan Swann's novels. Or I might write about being like one of the ancient statues of the goddess Artemis of Ephesias, with multiple breasts all over my body.

From childhood on, we are taught to "tell the truth, be honest," but the imagination has its own truth. These "lies" may shed light on another side of you, what Jungian psychologists call the Shadow, the thing that *you* would *never dare* to do or be. These lies may well tell the truth.

❉

Sexuality and the Erotic

> Warm sheets
> Empty bed —
> I smell her pillow.
> — Gina Shelton, "Dyku"

SEXUALITY IS SURELY, to adapt a phrase from Margaret Laurence, "the river that runs both ways." Sex can be a joyful, healing release, an expression of love and intimacy, enjoyment of good-natured lust, connection of souls as well as bodies and certainly the way to create children. Or it can be violent, abusive, toxic with shame and guilt. Surely we could imagine different words for these contrasting aspects of sexuality. Compare these two poems:

> ON LAKE JOSEPH
> (a.e.t.)
>
> tonight i give thanks for
> rainy, fog swept nights
> for the thrumming pulse
> of water on the roof
> waves lapping at the boat house doors
>
> tonight i give thanks for
> ancient passion
> once young, insistent, burbling
> through all the veins and nerves
> delightful warmth

SEXUALITY AND THE EROTIC

rosy communion of thighs and lips
in all the branches of our blood

tonight i give thanks for
all the new loves
who hear the rain
in their own pulses
who feel the sweet tender
tapping in their hearts
who worship the goddess
in the only rite
she ever gave
us

tonight

— Gertrude Lebans, in *Intricate Countries:*
Women Poets from Earth to Sky

On Loving Men in Difficult Times

We are making love
   on a bed
     in front of a television
Earlier, on the news
the story of a little girl   age 6
   raped, her throat slashed
& (almost worse) she survived.
The shadow of the rapist's
metal cock
   moves across your own
for only a second
my urgent blood turns cold

   You ask me
   What's the matter?

— Ellen Jaffe, in *Intricate Countries:*
Women Poets from Earth to Sky

South

In the first poem, the narrator gives thanks for the erotic experience. She perceives the natural world and other lovers as joining in the passion and tenderness that she and her lover share, now and in the past, and sees the moment as blessed by the goddess.

In the second poem, the scene of lovemaking is violated and desecrated by the news story about the child who was raped and by the woman's reaction to it. She sees her male lover (even if briefly) in the guise of the rapist. He widens the gulf between them by not being aware of this, asking "What's the matter?" Even the settings are different: making love "in front of a television" is less intimate than listening to falling rain and lapping water.

Erotic comes from the Greek word *eros*, "passionate love," life-promoting, creative, wild, energizing. Sexuality and the erotic have been repressed and distorted in many individuals, both women and men, and in much of society. Erotic is sometimes confused with pornographic. Pornography, trading in exploitation and surface titillation, is sterile and life-denying, as is excessive puritanism. Both these ways of looking at the world objectify and demean sexuality.

In her essay, "Uses of the Erotic: The Erotic as Power," Audre Lorde says, "The pornographic emphasizes sensation without feeling, while the erotic deals with our true, and strong, feelings." Thus pornography is actually a denial of the erotic. Lorde continues, "The erotic is a resource within each of us that lies in a deeply female and spiritual plane, firmly rooted in the power of our unexpressed or unrecognized feeling." She cautions women not to suppress their erotic nature in order to become "strong," because that would mean accepting a false idea of strength, "fashioned within the context of male models of power." (*Sister Outsider*, pp. 53-59)

Lorde extends the definition of erotic beyond its usual meaning. For her, the essence of the erotic is not only in sexuality; the erotic is also an inner sense of joy, satisfaction, loving what you do, including work, friendship, art, cooking, dance, gardening, children.

In a similar vein, Clarissa Pinkola Estes, in *Women Who Run with the Wolves*, describes the erotic as a deep wellspring of creative life, a combination of passion and compassion, love for the self and for the other, which is vital for both women and men.

Yet people too often act like the Greek king Penthius, in Euripides' play *The Bacchae*. Penthius, a man who lives by rigid rules of rationality, outlaws the musician Orpheus and his women-followers, the Bacchae — the forces of the erotic. The Bacchae then turn against Penthius with violence.

If we welcome the erotic into our lives, it can be a source of replenishment and renewal, able to heal the hurts we sustain in the course of our lives; if we shut it out, it can hurt us in some insidious way, or even harm others. Sometimes people block out any sexual or romantic experience because of past hurt and pain, as in this remark made by someone I know: "I've been burnt so often, I don't ever want to be warm again." But that leads to a cold life, and a cold heart. If sexuality has been fraught with danger, anger and suffering, then any new sexual or intimate feelings (and sometimes any feelings at all) may seem overwhelming, the enemy to be avoided at all cost. Can we learn to warm up gradually, without getting burnt again? Or to find that erotic fulfilment in other areas of life, as Audre Lorde suggests?

For Lorde, "the aim of each thing which we do is to make our lives and the lives of our children richer and more possible. With the celebration of the erotic in all our endeavours, my work becomes a conscious decision — a longed-for bed which I enter gratefully and from which I rise up empowered."

The erotic is feared, she adds, because once we begin to feel deeply and authentically, we begin to demand joy from the whole of our lives and look at all of life differently. We look more honestly at our lives to see what they offer of joy, meaningfulness and responsibility, and do not want to settle for "the shoddy, the conventionally expected, nor the merely safe."

South

Accepting the erotic takes courage. We must learn how to say *yes* to life as well as *no* to the things that deal death. Lorde talks about learning not "to fear the yes within ourselves." Jane Rule, in the film *Fiction and Other Truths*, says that we have done a great deal to educate children about not being abused sexually (how to say no), but we still do very little teaching about the positive values of sex and sexuality (how to say yes) for both gay and straight people. Until recently, societal condemnation made it especially difficult for lesbians and gay men to accept and to write about their sexuality. Now, however, "the love that dare not speak its name" flourishes in the pages of both specialized and mainstream literature.

Humour is another important element of the erotic. This does not mean jokes that are demeaning or cruel, but cleansing, full-bellied laughter. Clarissa Pinkola Estes talks about this in *Women Who Run with the Wolves*. She mentions the "belly-goddess" Baubo, who makes Demeter laugh while she is searching for her daughter Persephone, captured by the god of the underworld. Demeter, goddess of the earth, was so grief-stricken she had made all nature barren. The encounter with Baubo gives Demeter the will to go on searching, find her daughter and obtain her release. Even though Persephone had eaten several pomegranate seeds, causing her to go back to the underworld every winter, Demeter can now wait out that time in peace, knowing Persephone will return, spring will come and the cycle of life will continue. And Persephone, perhaps, learns something from her time away. Being taken to the "underworld" may also be seen as a retreat to the "inner world," a journey to the deeper recesses of herself, just as bulbs winter underground before blossoming in spring.

So, how do we begin to write about sexuality and the erotic? How do we free ourselves to put what we have been told is unspeakable, even unthinkable, into words and images? If much of the language of sex is "dirty words," how do we reclaim these words, dirt and all, and grow our garden?

EXERCISES

1. Finding an Image

Find an image for your joyful erotic nature. Audre Lorde pictured it as the drop of bright yellow food-colour mixed with pale margarine that was used during the Second World War. Therapist and writer Marion Woodman says that an image brings together mind and body, emotion and spirit; it leads us to the healing power of *imagination*, which can transform the way we look at our lives. If you cannot imagine having a joyful erotic nature now, think of what it might be like if you did have one. Remember that, as in Audre Lorde's definition, the erotic can include sexuality, but can also encompass passion, delight and freedom in the world as a whole.

Take this image as far out, and as deep in, as it will go. Write about it. Draw it, or find a picture that suggests it to you. The erotic affects and includes all our senses. Sometimes, drawing the picture first will suggest the words you want to use; sometimes, words will come before the picture. Or, if you like, dance the image or play music (recorded music or your own instrument, such as a drum or guitar) that suggests erotic images and feelings.

2. The First Time

Write about your first sexual experience or the first (or any) sexual experience in which you felt you had free choice as an equal and willing participant. Another way to look at this might be to write about the first time you felt you were truly in your sexual body, not just "having sex."

A variation would be to write a different ending to one of your sexual experiences. Write what you wish had happened, perhaps beginning your piece with the words "If only ..." Writing cannot undo the facts of the past, but it can provide a potential alternative, and inhabiting that imaginative space is healing and empowering.

South

3. Like Water for Chocolate

In this "magic realist" novel (later a film), certain everyday objects are imbued with special power. A dish of quail with rose petals, for example, quickly becomes an aphrodisiac on a huge scale. Write about an everyday, not explicitly sexual, experience in erotic terms, e.g., swimming in the ocean, eating a brownie or a peach, plucking a rose. Exaggerate some of the elements, or simply describe the experience, using all your senses. What do you see, hear, taste, touch, smell? How do you move? Have fun with this!

Here is an example:

QUIVERING

Eventually there was no stopping me. Those wild rosehips grabbed my mind then pulled me over. On the morning when I broke down and lost my resistance I grabbed the pruning snips. All I really wanted was to roll those lovely, shiny, red pearls between my index finger and thumb. The snips were a decoy.

I felt my eardrums tense as I twirled the first little berry. It was part of a healthy cluster of seven. The bush stood elegantly poised, dangling its juicy bits.

I smoothed these perfect gems between my urgent finger tips. Longing for your touch — for your rare touch. For so many months I've carried the memory of your knuckles gently pressed to my lips. My lips held that warm impression for days.

— Renee Sagebear, excerpt, "Quivering," in *Bite Me*

4. Sex Education

What messages were you given about sex as a child, both verbally and non-verbally? Who taught you — your parents? other children? other adults? animals/nature? What and how would you tell your own children, or children who come to you for guidance about sex? How would your message be different from what you learned? Write this as a letter or as a memory piece beginning "I Remember" *or* "I Don't Remember."

CHILDREN

My son, my daughter: May you never
be deaf to love.
— Anne Michaels, *Fugitive Pieces*

LIKE UKRAINIAN DOLLS, with smaller dolls nesting inside ever-larger ones, our childhoods are always with us. It is a paradox, but true, that writing about sad times can bring relief and peace. In addition, the more we can remember, even of sad things, the more memories of happier times come back too. Filling in missing pieces of the puzzle can make us more whole.

There has been much written about one's inner child. This may be the actual child you used to be, or simply the child in the adult, the potential to be spontaneous, alive with wonder, living in the moment. By nurturing and loving children in the present, we can also give a hand (and a hug) to our inner child.

Some of us have given birth to children and many others of us have children in our lives — children or grandchildren through marriage, nieces and nephews, children of friends and neighbours, children we teach or work with. Children can give us a second chance, a new hope. If there were traumatic events in our childhood, seeing children the same age we were when these events occurred may bring back painful memories. At the same time, knowing, loving and being involved with children can help us heal. We see that we have survived, even thrived, that life goes on. We also see that life can be different, that patterns can change.

South

If you had an especially difficult childhood, you may be tempted to be bitter at the unfairness of having been hurt as a child. Instead of following this kind of thought to a dead end, you can acknowledge it, write it in your journal and let it flow downstream, like a leaf on the current of your mind.

Another way to deal with these feelings is to write a story about a character who feels life has treated her unfairly, and let her wreak havoc in fiction, not in real life. As you intensify her bitterness and anger or her loneliness, you may find some warmer feelings underneath, discover or create another character who can comfort her, perhaps provide a magic gift or help her work towards some solution for her problem. Sometimes, just acknowledging that the problem can't be simply fixed, that she can't easily "get over it," is helpful. You will probably feel better for writing her down, out of your head.

It is also possible, through looking at old photographs and at toys you had as a child, visiting an old house or talking to family members, to put together memories and impressions in a new way, to *re-member* a life that has seemed scattered, even dismembered.

Even if you had a "good" childhood, there are lots of little hurts and bumps along the way. Remembering one detail can lead to others, and recreating those details *in the safety of the present* can give meaning to the past. We often put experiences in closed boxes in the closet of our minds, labelling them without really exploring or sorting through the contents, probably because those experiences (large or small) were things we could not cope with at the time. Remembering specific details takes away the labels of "good" and "bad" and helps us see the experience as well as ourselves and other people in all their complexity. We can let ourselves feel the sadness, anger, pleasure and confusion we were not allowed to feel at the time, or that we have just forgotten in the hustle of growing up.

Sometimes other family members recall events quite differently than we do; each of us is sure our version is correct.

CHILDREN

This can be interesting or curious if the event is benign and reveals something about the dynamics of family life. If there has been abuse or other major trauma, however, this memory-gulf can lead to conflict and feelings of not being validated or believed. It is important to stay with the memories you have, but sometimes telling the story to a new person, in another setting, can provide some new insights. Lenore Terr, a psychiatrist who has studied memory and trauma, tells the story of a little girl who remembered being sexually abused by her grandfather. Although this *might* have happened, retelling her story helped the girl and her mother remember that, at age three, the child had a painful examination for a urinary infection by a doctor who looked like her grandfather, and this was probably the source of the memory.

In other situations, however, memories of abuse are real and undeniable, no matter how much other people do not want to admit this. The healing work comes in accepting what has happened and finding ways to go on with your life. I will discuss issues of abuse more fully in the chapter on "Trauma."

In writing workshops, preteen children often go back to experiences of earlier childhood: a child will write about how she felt when Grandpa died or when the family moved house. Sometimes parents and other adults aren't able to talk to children at the time of these events, or don't know how. At other times, parents try to explain, but the child is too young to process the situation. Sometimes a child has an experience that she just can't communicate to anyone at the time, even something as simple as sleeping in a tent, hearing the trees blowing in the wind, watching the full moon. According to Lenore Terr, verbal memories develop at about thirty-six months, and most of our childhood "story memories" date from that time, although children have body memories or perception memories from earlier. My nephew, for example, was in hospital for severe allergies when he was just over one year old. Two years later, his mother put on, for the first time since the hospital, a

South

flowered blouse she had worn during their stay. He screamed at her to take it off, although he did not know why. Fortunately, she was able to make the connection and explain it to him.

If there are chunks of your childhood you don't remember, you might follow Natalie Goldberg's technique of beginning a writing exercise with the words "I don't remember ..." and then find that images and words come after all. You might focus on one specific year or one specific place where you lived, for this sort of exercise. You might need to use your support systems if the writing brings up distressing memories.

Yet children understand that sad stories need to be told and respond appropriately to those told by their peers. Most children know that neither the world of real life nor of imagination is always happy. One nine-year-old boy told me how it broke his heart when a character in the *Harry Potter* series was killed, but that made the book better. Another boy wrote about his two grandfathers who had died, saying " I knew I had to talk about my grandfathers, but I didn't know I could write a poem about them."

Other painful memories might stem from unintentional hurts. Children have creative spirits and love making things, but they need to be nurtured. Sometimes, though, adults can unintentionally wound a child's creativity. This excerpt from a poem I wrote based on a friend's childhood memory expresses this kind of hurt.

> MEMORY KICKS YOU IN THE TEETH AGAIN
> (or Intimations of Oppression on Recollection of Early Childhood—with apologies to William Wordsworth)
>
> When he was six
> he drew Jesus
> > green as grass
> alive/dead upon the cross
> with brand-new crayola crayons,
> proudly showed it to his class

CHILDREN

> they told him NO
>   Sunday-school teacher
>   minister
>   parents
> you can't make Jesus green
> as your feelings
>   spring leaves
>   or little apples under the tree ...
>
> — Ellen Jaffe, in *Apparitions:*
> *Visions from the Millennium*

EXERCISES

1. *The First Times ...*

Childhood is a time of firsts. Try some or all of these:
I remember/don't remember the first time I ate ice cream
    the first time I went swimming
    the first day of school, or the first day at a new school
    my first bike
    the first time I slept away from home
    moving to a new house
    my seventh (or tenth or thirteenth) birthday

2. *Childhood Dreams*

Dayal Kaur Khalsa, a Canadian writer and illustrator of children's books, wrote *Cowboy Dreams* when she was ill with cancer. She tells about wanting to be a cowboy as a little girl, believing, still, that a girl could be a cowboy. Not having a real horse, she used the basement bannister, with stirrups made from clothesline and toilet-paper rolls, and sang cowboy songs. What were your dreams as a child? How, in your imagination, did you make them come true? How did the people around you react to your dreams? What has happened to them now?

South

3. "Once Upon a Time ..." (Or "Cric-Crac" in Haitian)

Books and storytelling are important to most children. Make a list of some stories or songs you loved as a child. Do scenes or images from these stories come back to you as you live your life?

Write a story for children, based either on your own experience or imagination or on a retelling of a favourite story or legend. You can add pictures (drawings, collages, even cut-up photographs). Perhaps you have done this already for a child you know, either in writing or in storytelling. Telling stories is an art in itself and it is important to keep this oral tradition alive. If you have told many stories, write at least one as a book or picture book. Then try it out on a few children, in a big comfortable armchair or under a tree.

This exercise will, of course, take more time than fifteen minutes. You can work on it over several days or weeks, perhaps alternating with other writing.

4. *Being a Parent (or not)*

There are so many things to write about this subject, and it's easy to fall into the trap of sentimentality. Write a one-to-two-page article on how having a child, or not having a child, has changed your life.

In the years after my son's birth, I had two miscarriages and eventually found myself writing about that. I cannot give you an exercise for this kind of loss, but I did feel better being able to put it into words. One of the poems is included later in the book, in the section on death. I also wrote a long poem, "The Night Baby," about one of my son's seemingly endless crying spells, imagining he had been replaced by a changeling in the night; this helped me get some perspective on the situation, both his fears and my own "bad mother" feelings.

If you have had dealings with the medical technology of childbirth, or the social services system, writing about it might make you feel more human and empowered.

Animals

> Come into animal presence.
> — Denise Levertov, *Intimate Nature*

THE WORD *ANIMAL* IS DERIVED from the Latin word *anima*, meaning "soul" and "life," so it is ironic that western patriarchal tradition has denied souls to the animals we see and live with every day. In the Middle Ages, church fathers had long debates on this subject, concluding that animals had no souls and could not enter heaven. Adam's role was to "have dominion" over the animals in the garden.

This doctrine notwithstanding, men, women and children have always had close relationships with animals. To Aboriginal people around the world, animals are a sacred part of nature, like trees, stones, stars and the earth itself. Animals have spirits and are actively involved in creation stories and other myths and legends: Raven, Coyote and White Buffalo are notable examples. Raven, although sometimes a trickster, saves the people by stealing back the light from an old man who has stolen the light of the sun, moon and stars, and hoarded it away. Coyote is also a trickster, and an agent of change and disruption; he helps people laugh at themselves and break the bubble of vanity and pride.

In Greek and Roman myths and in many European fairy tales from pre-Christian times, we also see the closeness between humans and animals. People could transform from one to the other and back. (See Ovid's *Metamorphoses* and the

South

Grimm Brothers' fairy tales.) Sometimes these transformations referred to parts of human nature, such as sexuality and aggression, that were seen as more animal-like; think of the princes who turned into frogs and bears and had to be kissed (and, of course, loved) by a beautiful maiden to become human again. *Beauty and the Beast* typifies this story, although it also involves romantic stereotypes.

Animals connect us with earth as mother and with instinctual, physical, sensual parts of ourselves. Paradoxically, they also connect us with spirit. Shamans have "power animals" who help them in their work, and people can ask a shaman to find their own power animal (or learn how to find one for themselves) to give them energy and renewed life. First Nations people in Canada, like other peoples around the world, have animal clans and totems; each clan animal is a living presence with its own meaning. The Chinese calendar is divided into twelve-year cycles, each year in the cycle governed by a particular animal.

Writing about animals can encompass symbolic and imaginary creatures, as well as pets and wild animals we encounter in real life. My own limited experiences with animals are vivid in my mind. I lived in an apartment in New York when I was growing up, and my parents did not want to have a dog or a cat, though I did have a pet budgie. But there were the neighbours' two cocker spaniels, pigeons in the park and worms under stones. There were the animals in Central Park Zoo, elephants and camels. There was also a sad and lonely polar bear with dingy fur, living in a small cage with a puddle of water. This zoo, like others in the world, has recently been redesigned to improve the living conditions of the animals. Nonetheless, the subject of animals living in captivity is a difficult one for many, and something you might want to explore through writing. Surely we all have memories of animals that we can write about, showing the bond that people and animals share.

Sometimes, however, the experiences we have with animals are unpleasant or dangerous. Patricia Tighem wrote about

ANIMALS

being attacked by a grizzly bear in a recent book, *The Bear's Embrace*. In the chapter on "Trauma," we will look at a woman writing about a crocodile attack

Women have often had a special relationship with animals. *Intimate Nature: The Bond Between Women and Animals* (Hogan, Metzger and Peterson) includes stories, essays, meditations and poems by more than seventy women. Some of these women have spent their lives as writers, while others, like Jane Goodall, use writing to describe their primary work of observing, living and working with animals.

You can also write directly from an animal's point of view. I remember reading Anna Sewell's *Black Beauty* when I was about eight and being moved by the horse's-eye view of life. Barbara Gowdy, who looks with a unique eye at human beings, has also written from the point of view of elephants in her novel *The White Bone*. In Kim Echlin's *Elephant Winter*, a young woman learns and records the vocal language of the elephants with whom she works.

The desire and ability to communicate is one of the important things we share with animals. Whales and dolphins have songs or sonar; birds sing; bees dance; wolves howl; even the beaver slapping its tail on the water seems to be giving some kind of message. There have been many experiments trying to teach animals, usually primates, to communicate in human language, such as American Sign Language. Sometimes these animals are in laboratories; sometimes a chimpanzee is raised in a home, like a human child. These studies are intriguing, but I would rather we communicate with animals as creatures free to live their own lives.

Helping an animal through a crisis can be a powerful experience. Sandy Kenny, writing from a farm in Pennsylvania, describes the long and harrowing but rewarding experience of being alone at lambing time during a blizzard. In this excerpt from her journal, one ewe has given birth to tiny triplets but is not able to feed them, while another ewe is mourning twin lambs who died in the snow:

South

> I take them to the barn every hour, and repeat the efforts to get them to suckle. Each attempt is more difficult; the mother balks now even when I touch her, the lambs blindly push against her, unable to find her warm sustaining teat, and then in despairing weakness fall to the straw and lie motionless. Exhausted, I sit in the corner of the pen and close my eyes, tears squeezing out from under my eyelids. Gradually I become aware of the soft breath and gentle voicing from the next pen where the lambless mother is isolated. Cautiously I hold up one of the triplets so she can smell it. I wait for her to nudge it forcefully away as she gets the scent of the baby's real mother. To my amazement, she begins to nuzzle and coo as the lamb makes a small cry. I move to her pen, holding the baby against me, and slowly position the lamb against her udder. She nickers again softly, and sniffs at the lamb, then smells me all over. As I guide the lamb's mouth to her nipple, she stands calmly, and looks at me deeply as if trying to memorize my face, and allows the baby to nurse. Encouraged, I try another of the three. She gently welcomes this one too!

Kenny combines closely observed detail about the sheep with describing her own feelings. The reader, like Kenny herself, becomes more aware of how sheep behave and react.

You can also write about imaginary animals like the unicorn or about events that may never take place. Marion Engel's novel *Bear* is, in a way, the opposite of stories in which a human turns temporarily into an animal. In this story, a woman, alone on a northern island, develops a relationship for a while with a bear, who remains a real bear despite his connection with the human. The transformation takes place within the woman herself.

Transformation is a common theme in animal stories. There is an ancient myth, with Celtic, Siberian, Scottish, Northwest Indian and Inuit variations, of a seal-woman who comes on land and has her seal skin stolen by a man whom she then marries and to whom she bears children. Eventually, she begins to pine away, discovers her hidden skin, puts it on and swims back to her home, leaving her children behind or perhaps taking one with her for a visit or forever. One telling of this story appears in *Women Who Run with the Wolves*; filmmaker John Sayles gives another version in *The Secret of Roan Inish*. We can see the seal-woman as a metaphor for our own need to be connected to our true self and to nature. Cut off from that connection, we die emotionally and spiritually.

Exercises

1. *Pet Show*

Write about the first pet you remember having or a pet you wished you could have. What kind of animal was it? What was its name? How did you get it? What did you do together? And (if it's no longer alive) how did it die? Or write about a pet that you have now, or one you would like to have.

2. *Being an Animal*

Think about the poem you wrote in the "Who Am I?" chapter. One of the questions was, What animal would you be? Choose that animal, or another one, and write about what it would really feel like to be that animal. Where would you be? What would you do? Who would your friends be? You can try moving or dancing as if you were this animal, before you write about it: find a space, indoors or outdoors, where you feel comfortable doing this. It helps take you out of your head and into the nature of the animal (whether it swims, walks or flies).

3. *Reaching Out to an Animal*

Have you ever had an experience of actually helping an animal in some way, saving it from harm, helping it give birth or survive being orphaned? Write about what that was like for you. Then, write about that experience from the animal's point of view.

South

4. *Animal Spirit*

If you have a particular animal, like a clan or totem animal, that is special, sacred or connected to you, and you feel comfortable writing about its meaning in your life, do that. You might want to draw the animal and write your poem or prose piece inside or alongside the picture.

❖

West

Autumn
Water
Sunset
Going inward, entering darkness
Emotions, Dreams, Personal Truths
Finding a goal that has meaning

> *Autumn tiptoes in*
> *Cornstalks edged in brown*
> *Goosebumps in the air.*
>
> — GINA SHELTON
> "Seasons"

EMOTIONS

... What a gamble to let feelings become deep! It doesn't matter what you feel as long as you feel, and to be a writer and have to record the details of this ultimate gamble, a small ship on a stormy sea ...

— David McFadden, "Malcolm Lowry," *The Art of Darkness*

STRONG EMOTIONS ARE THE LIFEBLOOD of writing. I used to keep by my computer a cartoon that read: "It's easy to be a writer. Just open a vein and begin." At university, I was taught that poetry is, in Wordsworth's phrase, "emotions recollected in tranquillity." In the same sentence, Wordsworth also described poetry as "a spontaneous overflow of feeling." I think sometimes the writing comes before, and may even bring about, the tranquillity. Any emotions you can translate into words are a starting point.

The author's emotion affects the reader too. In a creative writing workshop for teens, one girl remarked, "When I read poems, sometimes I have the same feelings, even though I'm not in the same situation." She was talking about empathy, the ability to project yourself, for the moment, into the feelings of someone else. We were reading aloud poems from the book *I Never Saw Another Butterfly*, poetry and drawings by children in Terezein concentration camp during the Second World War — poems that still had the power to reach the hearts of children in Brantford, Ontario, in the year 2000.

West

This book is an extreme example, both of artwork created in a time of utter hardship and fear (similar, in its own way, to the making of quilts in the south), and of the power of this artwork to affect people far removed from that situation. We use our own emotions to connect with the feelings of these children who express their hopes, memories, terror, and their perceptions of beauty as well as pain.

We also use our emotions to connect to the feelings experienced by adults. I remember reading *A Reckoning*, a novel by May Sarton, and crying freely at the scene in which the narrator's beloved friend is dying. My (then) husband came into the room and remarked, "Why do you want to read a book that makes you cry?"

Why indeed? It is a valid question. I think part of the answer is that, by sharing feelings, we realize we are not so alone in the universe. In addition, there is a kind of pleasure in vicarious feeling — this death, for instance, has not really happened in our own lives, and yet it is real. This is not ghoulish or macabre but an extension and deepening of our own humanity. As readers, we have already experienced the death of friends, or we will need to deal with death at some time in our lives. While novels are not self-help books, a good novel can often help us learn about life by entering imaginatively into the characters' lives. We can also empathize with the characters' love, happiness and joy, and learn more about those feelings.

For writers, the writing process helps us discover and understand our feelings, about ourselves and other people, about nature, about the world. I think we do not write *about* feelings so much as we write *from a place of feeling*. It is a process of discovery, exploring *terra incognita*. Whether we are writing about ourselves and people we know, or about a character we have created, good writing can give us that sense of touching the core of something true, the feeling you get when you split a piece of wood in exactly the right place, exposing the heart. To carry the metaphor further, these pieces of wood can turn into

EMOTIONS

a fire that gives us light and warms us, burning away the inessential and illuminating the darkness.

"In the destructive element immerse yourself," Joseph Conrad wrote in *Lord Jim*. As writers, we need to develop the art of immersing ourselves without drowning, and without getting the bends when we surface. The experience of writing is a journey that takes us from one feeling to another; and sometimes it is surprising where we end up. We may start writing in anger and find it leads to sadness, or begin in despair that leads to anger or joy.

If we can contain in words such feelings as hate, vengefulness or jealousy, we may not need to act them out in our daily lives. This may be what a friend meant when he advised me, long ago, that the best place for selfishness is in writing. Selfishness may be reframed as the need to care for and respect *ourselves*, our needs and our boundaries. Once we do this, we can also respect other people's needs and boundaries. As I have noted, women especially have a hard time seeing ourselves as "selfish," because our traditional role is to help and care for others. This is not wrong in itself; life depends on our helping each other. But it can be carried to extremes. We often tell ourselves, "I *should* do this or that." Bonnie Filipchuk, a counsellor whom I worked with, suggested substituting "I *could*..." for "I *should*." When I try this, it makes me feel much lighter, a weight taken off my shoulders.

We often write from painful emotions: anger, fear, grief, pain, confusion, shame, guilt, remorse. Finding images and stories for the feelings can make them bearable. A black hole, a storm-tossed sea, a moth against a flame — the strength of these images can take us to unforeseen places. Ursula K. LeGuin says that imagery "takes place in 'the imagination'... the meeting place of the thinking mind with the sensing body. What is imagined isn't physically real, but it *feels as if it were:* the reader sees or hears or feels what goes on in the story, is drawn into it, exists in it, among its images, in the imagination (the reader's?

the writer's?) while reading." ("Where Do You Get Your Ideas From?" p. 196)

Tears are a river that takes you somewhere (Clarissa Pinkola Estes, *Women Who Run with the Wolves*) — and anger is the fire that keeps you going. We need to keep anger hot, keep it from becoming the ice of resentment and bitterness. Sometimes poems or stories written out of anger are frightening, to yourself and to others who read them. Being "good girls," we backtrack: "Oh I'm sorry, I didn't mean that." Have the courage to stand by the anger in the writing and look at where it comes from. Writing about anger does not mean that you will act it out. Anger might, however, give you newfound energy to change your life and the world around you. It is scary to do this, and it is scarier if we do not.

Sometimes it is harder to write from a place of happiness. We may have less to say, or believe we are tempting fate by talking about our good fortune. But it is also important to let ourselves feel these feelings and find words and images to celebrate joy, love, even fun.

Humour is also an important tool in writing about emotions. Humour gives us distance and perspective, and although sometimes we need to be close to strong feelings, sometimes we can take a few steps away and use a gentle humour to deal with a difficult situation.

It may help to find a form for the feelings. William Butler Yeats wrote that poetry is "meaning in a cage of form," and this applies to prose too. The meaning is not *trapped* in the cage but *contained* in it. The form can involve metre, pattern or the repetition of key phrases. "Once upon a time," we begin, and end with "They lived happily ever after." In Haiti, a traditional storyteller calls out "Cric?" to the audience when she or he wants to begin the story, and the audience responds "Crac!" if they want to hear. Only then can the storyteller begin.

After great pain, a formal feeling comes, wrote Emily Dickinson. This line of poetry became the title for the book,

EMOTIONS

A Formal Feeling Comes: Poems in Form by Contemporary Women, dealing with ways that poetic forms can be used today. It is a good place to start learning about this subject, as is Mary Oliver's *A Poetry Handbook*. The discipline of metre, rhyme, number of lines and so on can enclose strong emotion, and poetry is crafted in the tension between these two elements.

We often feel overwhelmed and helpless in the face of news stories of tragedy and despair. Some of these touch us more deeply than others. Sometimes we can take direct action, such as protesting at a demonstration or making a donation to a worthwhile cause; sometimes, however, we need to express in writing, art or music our feelings about an incident, seemingly unrelated to us, that has touched our lives. We may write from our own point of view, as an outsider, or from the perspective of a participant in the situation.

Here is an example from my own work. I, like many people, was horrified and fascinated by the story of Susan Smith, the South Carolina woman who pushed the car holding her two young sons into a lake, drowning them. Without consciously deciding to write a poem about her, the words came and I was writing from Susan Smith's point of view. I could not, of course, know what she felt when she pushed the car into the water or after her arrest, but I could draw on my own feelings as a mother, my feelings towards Susan, and my wondering what would it be like to be this person.

REQUIEM
for Michael and Alexander Smith, and Susan Smith:
November 6, 1994

It is all there, John D. Long Lake
   red car, muddy road,
the children in their car-seats
sticky with popsicles and pee

West

the three-year-old can talk now
    where are we going mommy?
    are we there yet?
the baby's too young to speak
but sings a lullaby
to his teddy bear
plans go round in her head
    like wheels stuck in the mud
    red mud of the south
    her life
    stuck in the mud
    but where does she think she'll go,
how far will she get
on her made-up story of kidnapping?
    tell me a story, mommy
I remember my son at three,
    the endless stories,
    three little plums
    invited to eat dinner with the fox
    and rescued by their mommy —
    just in time.
she pushes the car — maybe someone will see —
but no one comes to save her, or save them
her little fishes stuck in their safety-net,
their watery grave

    did they cry much,
    she wonders now

    did Michael call for her?
    did Alexander scream?
    will they have nightmares in their endless sleep?

the lightbulb burns her eyes but still
the bad dreams haunt her

EMOTIONS

>she is drowning, drowning and she cannot swim
>the lake grows cold, colder, slowly
>she turns to ice
>the fishes' tongues stick to her when they lick
>and they all have blue eyes and blond hair.

This poem takes the writer and the reader to a very dark place, but such stories can also lead us back to the light, like Ariadne's thread through the Cretan labyrinth. Kate Halliday, a writer and therapist in Ithaca, New York, has commented that a writer "makes you look at people you'd rarely see and shines them up and loves them for the reader." Furthermore, although "writers of murder mysteries (are) not necessarily murderers," in Jane Rule's words, the writer uses her own feelings as a key to gain entry into other people's worlds, alien as these may appear.

One aspect of writing is bearing witness to events in the world. American poet Carolyn Forché has edited a collection called *Against Forgetting: Twentieth-Century Poetry of Witness*, a wide-ranging selection of international poems that cover the many horrors of this century, but that are always imbued with a deep and undying love of life. For me, the best political writing starts with ordinary personal details juxtaposed against a larger backdrop. In this kind of work, the personal is political, and the political is personal. Writing in a creative, not polemical, way about events that seem both horrific and meaningless may keep alive a sense of compassion, and may save us from feeling relentlessly angry, or helpless and numb. Lorna Crozier captures this in her poem "Without Hands," cited in the chapter "Talking to Your Body."

There is a true story about Anna Akhmatova, a Russian poet whose works were banned during the Stalinist terror, and who risked persecution for continuing to write on scraps of paper while her friends learned her poems by heart. She was standing in line outside a prison in Leningrad, waiting to visit a friend inside, when a woman behind her, who had probably never heard of Akhmatova's poems, asked in a whisper if she could put this terror into words. "And I said, 'I can,'" she recalled later. (Amanda Haight, *Anna Akhmatova: A Poetic Pilgrimage*, p. 99)

Songwriters, especially in the twentieth century, have found ways of expressing ideas of social injustice and outrage in music, using melody and rhythm as well as words to give form to their feelings. Especially when sung in groups, songs give people a sense of community and common purpose.

It is, I think, important to be aware of the ever-shifting balance between our private and public lives. Like a Moebius strip, each turns and flows into the other.

EXERCISES

1. *Going Fearward*

First, write a list of your fears, about five to ten of them. They can be small or large. Now, choose one of the fears and write a love poem — to a lover, child, parent, friend, even the world — using that fear as the central image. (I am indebted for this exercise to Marybeth Rua-Larsen.)

2. *Joy and Hope*

Joy and a sense of hope are not "somewhere over the rainbow," but in the small miracles of daily life. List your joys, small and large. Choose one to write about more deeply, as a poem or prose piece. Then keep a list of joys you discover every day for a week. At the end of the week, write about the experience of recording your joys. Could you do this for a month? Can it become part of your writing life, your practice?

EMOTIONS

3. *Could and Should*

Draw a vertical line down the centre of your page. On the left, write five sentences about yourself using *should* (e.g., "I should exercise more"). Now, on the right, write each sentence again, substituting *could* for *should* ("I could exercise more"). Note how this change makes you feel.

Do the exercise again, for other people in your life. (My son should/could study more; my partner should/could do more things with me). How does this feel? Which seems to give you more options, "should" or "could"?

4. *"I Read the News Today"*

Listen, watch and read the news. Notice which events touch you most deeply. Write a response to one of them, either to the event directly or to a memory it evokes in you. Sometimes it is not the news in the headline but the human interest story on an inside page that will catch your eye. Even obituaries and birth notices can provide food for the imagination.

A lighter variant of this exercise is to buy a tabloid newspaper at the corner store. Find a story that intrigues you, and write from the point of view of one of the characters in the story. (Most of these are made up, anyway, so you won't be changing "the facts").

Trauma

> A book ought to be an ice-pick, to break up the frozen sea within us.
> — Franz Kafka

> Though life may be painful, there is a joy and a power in writing, even when you're dealing with something that is hard to live through day by day. You're trying to understand what you're living through by using the tools of words and the beautiful inner structure of language.
> — Sandra McPherson, cited in Bill Moyers, *The Language of Life*

Life has many painful experiences for us, as well as moments of joy and pleasure. Some of these are *traumatic*, defined as experiences that cause feelings of overwhelming shock and helplessness. Trauma can be caused by the actions of other human beings, individually or in groups (e.g., in wartime); by animals or weather — floods, earthquakes and other forces of nature; by illness; by machines (cars, airplanes, even normally innocuous machines such as toasters). Traumas can range from experiencing the sudden death of a loved one, to a serious injury, to being raped or kidnapped. Grief often accompanies trauma, but these two are not the same thing.

The after-effects of trauma, like the ripples of a stone thrown in a pond, are widespread and long-lasting. Shamans

TRAUMA

have long believed that in a traumatic experience, a part of a person's soul may actually split off and become lost; the person can still function, but may sense a void inside and feel unfulfilled, depressed or spaced-out. Restoring the soul and making the person (more) whole is part of the shaman's work. This can also be seen as a metaphor for the healing process. In *Intricate Countries: Women Poets from Earth to Sky*, M.B. Stacy writes about this process, and the marks it leaves:

> PAID IN FULL
>
> I am
> a member of
> the scar clan.
> I am
> one of many
> each unique
> the scars we carry
> I am
> healthy and strong
> despite the knives
> carving my flesh
> despite the words
> tearing my soul.
> They removed the
> organs deemed
> unnecessary.
> My body
> mourned the loss
> I've repaid
> the debt.
> I am
> a member of
> the scar clan
> no longer
> hide the marks
> the traces of bravery

the woman
I've become.

Shamans are sometimes called "wounded healers," showing that they are not immune from hurt but that they have overcome their own wounds enough to help others. Similarly, writing about an experience cannot change the fact that it happened, but it can change how we think and feel about it. It can help us see aspects of the experience we may not have noticed at the time, and can, perhaps, help us move from *living* the experience over and over to *thinking* about it as one part of our ongoing life story.

Fifteen-year-old Lisa remarked that she didn't like her social worker telling her that she had to keep talking about the abuse she had experienced. "I want to think about other things," she said. And yet, for two summers in my writing group, she wrote moving poems and stories dealing directly and obliquely with her experiences. "I am a person with deep dark secrets inside my soul ..." one poem began. Creative writing seemed different from talking to a counsellor about her life. Perhaps writing gave her a sense of control over her feelings and experiences and the satisfaction of creating and crafting something outside herself that communicated to others. Her writing showed a complex, multifaceted individual, not just a survivor of abuse.

Different people may react differently to the *same type* of traumatic event or even the *same event* (like a plane crash, or a kidnapping), because of both their own experiences and associations and their inborn temperament or personality. Medical research is beginning to understand the pathways by which trauma affects a person's whole being, physically, emotionally, even cognitively. This is often called "post-traumatic stress."

In the 1980s, psychologist J. Pennebaker studied the effects of writing about trauma. University students were divided into two groups: one group was asked to write about assigned topics dealing with trivial or daily events; the other group was asked to write about the most upsetting or traumatic event of their life, with the proviso that they write about their deepest thoughts and feelings regarding the event. They were told not to worry about spelling and grammar, and encouraged to write about experiences they had not previously talked about in detail. Each group wrote for four consecutive days, fifteen minutes per day.

In the most significant version of this study, the group writing about traumatic events was itself divided into three: one group was asked to describe the facts of what happened, the second was asked to vent their feelings, and the third was asked to do both. This last group experienced beneficial health effects, even six months later. In a paper describing these studies, Joshua Smyth, a colleague of Pennebaker, reported that students found writing about the traumatic experiences valuable and meaningful. They willingly engaged in writing, and even students who turned in poor term papers seemed to know intuitively how to make a coherent narrative of their own personal tragedy. Students did experience short-term emotional distress while writing, but over the next six months they used far fewer health services and their grades improved. They also felt better emotionally. In some cases, even their immune systems improved. These benefits were not brought about by any response to their writing, as they did not receive any feedback on it (although they did fill out questionnaires about the effects of this study). It was the act of writing itself that was healing. Pennebaker's own book, *Opening Up: The Healing Power of Confiding in Others*, discusses his work in more detail, as do his more academic papers. He notes that he was surprised to find so many "profound human tragedies" among a group of suburban college students.

In later research, Smyth found that people with rheumatoid arthritis and with asthma who wrote about traumatic events began to feel better subjectively and also showed clinical improvement in their health. Since then, many studies have confirmed these results, looking at both men and women in various countries, with differing language, cultural, health and educational backgrounds.

How does this healing take place? One possible explanation lies within the brain. Memories of traumatic events seem to be encoded differently than other events, perhaps under the influence of stress hormones. These memories, stored in the right hemisphere of the brain, take the form of vivid, fragmented sense memories (sight, sound, smell, taste, touch, even movement) and intense emotions. Smyth says that these traumatic memories seem to lack a verbal component; in technical terms, there is a decrease of activity in Broca's area of the brain, which is associated with speech and language. When the memories intrude into our minds as flashbacks, perhaps stimulated by triggers or subtle cues in the environment, we can become highly aroused and emotional.

During writing, however, the experiences are re-coded into narrative language, which modifies both the emotions and the vivid sense impressions of the memory. This continues to happen as we write repeatedly about a subject or experience. Good writing does not completely neutralize the experience: the emotions and impressions are still there, but in a form which is more thinkable, more bearable. In effect, the traumatic experience stays with us but the overwhelming feelings of the trauma subside or are transformed. Language and thought can cradle raw experience, letting it live, breathe, cry, in a safer, more contained place. Expression in art or writing may come years after the traumatic event, whether or not that event is remembered consciously.

In writing about these events, the capacity to bring together feelings and descriptive details is important. Trauma often splits the two. We may be flooded with feeling but remember few details about what actually happened. Or we may recite a description of the event as if it were a newspaper article but remain cut off from our feelings. If you cannot combine the two to begin with, you can start with only one detail, one impression, one vague feeling or image.

In *Don't: A Woman's Word*, her heart-stopping book about her childhood sexual abuse, Elly Danica recounts how, after isolating herself in a house in Saskatchewan to retreat and begin healing, she first remembered an image of light shining underneath a doorway. This led to further memories. It is important to take the image that you see (or hear, or smell) and write about it, to see what it says to you, even if you do not know where the image comes from or how it relates to the trauma.

I think that, in the act of writing, of putting pen to paper, you are not addressing a blank paper or wall, but an active, supportive listener, somewhere in the corner of your mind. In *Women Who Hurt Themselves: A Story of Hope and Understanding*, Dusty Miller imagines a "non-helpful bystander" who was there (in our minds, if not in reality) at the time a trauma took place, and asks that we replace this figure with a "helpful bystander" who can assist in the healing process. The "active listener" can serve this role: encouraging, giving feedback, taking in words without judging and giving new energy and awareness. Your journal is a non-judgemental listener, the opposite of the Inner Critic: naming your feelings to the journal usually lessens shame and makes things seem less catastrophic. (Some people may also need the support of a therapist or counsellor to deal with the feelings and memories aroused by this writing. If this is not feasible, perhaps there is a friend or family member you can rely on for a comforting shoulder and a listening ear.)

Patricia Tighem's book, *The Bear's Embrace*, mentioned in the chapter on "Animals," can also be cited here as an example of writing about surviving trauma. Tighem subtitles her book "the true story of surviving a grizzly bear's attack," which highlights how she has turned raw experience into a story. Her trauma involved not only the bear's attack itself but also the damage to her body, the flashbacks she experienced and even some aspects of medical treatment.

In another example of coping with an attack by an animal, Val Plumwood, an Australian philosopher and feminist and a skilled woodswoman, wrote about her near-fatal encounter with a crocodile in Kakadu National Park, in an article called "The Ultimate Journey." Plumwood says that it took almost ten years before she could tell her story on her own terms. And then each retelling "took part of the pain and distress of the memory away." The reader, too, can share some of these feelings and yet experience safety and relief, almost a rebirth, at the end of the story. Plumwood found that some people saw her as a helpless woman attacked and ravished by a monster, an interpretation untrue to her experience. She knew that the crocodile was a wild animal in its own habitat and that her skills in the bush helped her escape and survive.

Rape itself is a trauma that is often misinterpreted. It is a crime of assault and power, but the sexual nature of the assault can often mask this. This reaction by others (e.g., media, the legal system, even friends and family) can lead to shame and self-blame an after-effect of many kinds of trauma and abuse, even when the victim is clearly not at fault. We may find ourselves telling our story many times, in many different ways, partly to deal with these difficult feelings.

I have found this true of my own experience of being raped. I was teaching school at the time. Shortly after school closed for the day, I was still in the classroom marking papers when the intruder entered, saying he was looking for the adult education class.

I survived, but I was not able to think or write about the assault for sixteen years. Then I wrote a long poem in response to a friend's poem about a similar experience. Since then, it has come into my writing in various ways, both as the event itself (as I remember it) and as stories or poems about other women who were sexually assaulted. Sometimes we do not realize that our stories are about ourselves as well as other people. Years after my experience, I wrote a story about a woman raped and then stabbed to death by a hitchhiker whom she picked up on the highway. The story had a powerful effect on me, and I felt strangely better after I finished writing it. It was only later that I realized the story was also about my own fears. The young man who had attacked me had a small penknife, although he never used it, and ran away immediately after the rape itself. Marge Piercy talks about the blatant and insidious dangers of rape in her "Rape poem," which helped me in my healing.

At this point, you may be thinking, *I don't want to get that close to a traumatic experience.* And you may be right, especially if the event is recent. You have to decide what is right for you. If you don't want to write about a difficult experience you are going through, maybe you can make some simple notations about your day, including all the things you do that are *not* connected to the trauma. "Sunny today after a week of rain. Planted petunias." These ordinary moments may come back as good memories during a sleepless night.

We do not always choose to write about a traumatic event; sometimes it chooses us. In writing groups, we often select a seemingly innocuous subject: traffic, old shoes, sitting around the kitchen table, even a quote from a poem or story. But as you begin to write, an event or experience may surface that you had not intended to write about. If there is something on your mind, any topic may lead to it. We find ourselves writing what we need to say, and remembering what is necessary for our healing.

Exercises

Please make sure you have enough support around you to do these exercises, and remember to take care of your body while you write, making sure you are well-nourished and comfortable.

1. *Directed Writing*

If you feel up to it, use Pennebaker's and Smyth's format of describing your thoughts and feelings about a traumatic incident in your life. Write about this for fifteen minutes a day, for four days. Notice if there are any after-effects from this exercise on your emotions, your physical health, your performance at work, school or leisure activities, and your relationships with others.

2. *Third-Person Retelling*

Write a narrative about a traumatic or difficult experience, using the third person (she) rather than the first person (I). You can describe the events that happened to you, or you can make up a story about a similar experience happening to a fictional character. This helps distance you from the event.

3. *Healing*

Write about things that have helped you heal from a trauma. What, and who, was helpful? What else did you need? How could you help someone else in a similar situation?

4. *Talking Back*

Write a letter to a person or thing that has traumatized you. The trauma may be on a large or small scale. If it was a car accident, you could write to the car (yours or the other person's), or to the blizzard or snowy street. Perhaps it was a tornado, or a hurricane, or a grizzly bear. Although it may feel worse if it was a human being who hurt you (because you can ascribe blame, malice, deliberate intent), impersonal forces can also cause pain. Even if you know the tornado did not mean to blow your house down, you can still be left bereft and homeless.

This letter is not to be sent. It is a way to express your thoughts and feelings *to yourself*. Confronting a person who has traumatized you is a very different matter and needs to be done carefully and with support, if at all.

Dreams

> In dreams begin responsibilities.
> — Delmore Schwartz, *In Dreams Begin Responsibilities*

DREAMS ARE ALMOST ALWAYS part of sleep, although they often disappear into mist on waking. Sometimes, however, a dream is so vivid and real it demands your attention, and often signifies or accompanies some major change in life.

Several years ago I had such a dream. I was driving up a steep hill in a desert-like area when I ran over a cougar that had suddenly appeared. I drove a few metres further, then stopped the car and went back to attend to the wounded animal. I could see it was a female cougar, badly hurt but still alive. I decided that I needed to leave my enclosed van and stay with the animal, and I felt relieved and glad when she regained her strength. She then led me down a footpath I hadn't noticed before.

This dream came at a time when I was preparing to take a leave of absence from my job at a counselling agency to concentrate on teaching and writing. I was leaving the beaten track to pursue my own passion. I felt somewhat stifled in my work, but I was also having misgivings about leaving. Writing about the dream helped me realize that if I continued at work, thinking primarily about pleasing others, I would be wounding or killing my own spirit, represented by the cougar. Daring to face the cougar, who might be dangerous when wounded, and following her down the unexplored path were steps towards acknowledging my own feelings and needs. To do this, I had to leave the safety of my car, which cut me off from the world around me. Also, the car was cold metal, while the cougar was warm and alive.

Even if I had not been able to leave my job, this dream might have been telling me to pay more attention to the "cougar" aspects of myself, which could include physical needs, sexuality, the desire to take time to write and the courage to follow my own path.

No one really knows what dreams are. Freud viewed them as "the royal road to the unconscious"; other psychologists believe they are merely scraps of retained images or random neural firings in the brain, which the mind later constructs into a story. Regardless, some dreams seem merely odd and incoherent, while others, like my cougar dream, feel vivid and meaningful. Working with the latter kind can help you find your direction and notice things that are blocking your way. Writing down your dreams each morning can help you remember and think about them, and may even help you dream more clearly.

One school of thought says that everything in your dream is a part of yourself. It is also true that figures in dreams may have more than one meaning. After you describe the dream itself, you could write about what might happen next or consider the different aspects more fully. I could, for example, have written more about the cougar or imagined the walk down the footpath. Dreams work in images and symbols: the desert in my dream might have suggested that a part of my life was becoming barren and dry.

While working on this book, I had another dream, set in Central Park. It seemed to me that a "central" park may be that vital growing place at the *centre* of ourselves, a wilderness that is tamed enough to let us relax and play. A journal can be a park for the imagination, a space to dream and be free, to explore different aspects of your life without taking dangerous risks. Since I grew up in New York, the image of Central Park might

DREAMS

also refer to my childhood; someone else would not have this association.

Dreams give us a chance to be, for a brief time, someone different or to experience a different life. In this way they are like art or play. We also use the word *play* for dramatic works, where the actors "become" their characters and we willingly suspend disbelief, ready to spend an hour or two in the Forest of Arden or playing bingo with *The Rez Sisters* in Tomson Highway's play. When children play, they try out different roles and identities, even places, as if they were in another dimension.

Many stories are written as dreams, *Alice in Wonderland* and *Through the Looking Glass* being among the most famous; this allows the writer creative freedom, but still grounds the story in reality. Still, sometimes we wonder which is which – as Alice wonders, is the Red King part of her dream or is she part of his?

Dreams can also refer to waking hopes and goals and our responsibility and zeal to bring them to life, as in Martin Luther King's famous speech, "I have a dream."

Exercises

1. *Dreamwork*

Take a dream that calls attention to itself, as mine did. Write down the plot of the dream, then explore the images and their associations. Does this dream shed some light on a question or problem you are having? What kind of feelings did you have in the dream and upon waking? Then put yourself, awake, into the dreamscape. What will happen next? Is there something you can give or receive from one of the characters in the dream? Think of how your dream might be a coded language. I once dreamt about a house with *solar* heating and realized this also referred to the *soul*, and how to keep my soul-fire going.

2. *Flying or Falling*

Many people have had flying dreams and falling dreams. Without necessarily putting in the details of your dream, write one page, prose or poetry, titled "Falling" and another page titled "Flying." Think about colours, sounds, smells, how you would move, what you might encounter.

3. *Rest and Renewal*

Dreams, like sleep itself, often replenish and refresh us. For this exercise, you don't need to write anything. Take your writing time today and do something that fills you with wonder, contentment or joy, something that seems like *play*. *Play* comes from a word meaning "to dance, leap for joy, rejoice," but also "to have the care of, cultivate." Play is more than a diversion; it is vital to our ability to respond to life. Remember to do this frequently. In writing, we give out a great deal of ourselves, and we need to refill the well when it begins to run dry.

❖

Treats and Secrets

Secrets remind me of old ecru lace, tatted gracefully by gnarled, spotty hands with knuckles swollen through a lifetime's cold water and hard work. Secrets are akin to lies, and lies sink deeply into swamp-mud, covered for years until an enterprising barn-swallow burrows through the silt to construct a half-shell nest of mud and secrets on brown barn beams.

— Angela Hrabowiak, "Secrets"

I WAS WALKING PAST a flower shop in my neighbourhood one warm summer day when a woman about sixty-five or seventy came out carrying two carnations, cream and red, wrapped in gift paper. I had stopped to look at the plants displayed outside, but she may have thought I was looking at her and said, with a hint of apology but also pride in her voice, "Every week I give myself a little treat."

"That's wonderful," I said, "Enjoy!"

We walked on, in our opposite directions. I thought about how rarely women give ourselves that little treat, as simple and as beautiful as a fresh flower. We have all kinds of excuses: "It's too expensive, too much trouble, I don't deserve that." And I wonder whether many people knew about this woman's treat to herself, or whether she kept it a secret. It is sad that many of us have to wait until we are older to accept that gift from ourselves.

And yet, it is wonderful that we can learn to do that at any age. I remember the smile on the woman's face, the lilt of confidence in her voice. It is nice to get flowers and similar treats from other people, but it is also good to give and receive those special treats ourselves, to realize we are worth it. Perhaps, until we can love ourselves enough to do that, it is harder for other people to love us, or for us to really love others. It is a two-way street, however, because sometimes a gift from another person will make us feel valued enough to give to ourselves. Or, conversely, we may learn to give generously to ourselves by the pleasure of giving to others. It's all in getting the right balance.

I went to university at Wellesley, a women's college in Massachusetts, whose Latin motto was (and is) *Non sed ministrari sed minister*, "Not to be ministered to, but to minister," implying we were being educated for a life of service to the world and to our families. However, that motto seems to skew the balance we need in our lives. If we are always ministering we have nothing left to give ourselves or to receive from others, and we are always in a position of power— the one in control of the giving. In a balanced view of life that sees us as interdependent, connected in a kind of spiritual "worldwide web," we would both minister and be ministered to, as the need arises, in a flexible give-and-take. The need for something to make our spirit sing is lifelong. Allowing ourselves time and space to write and giving ourselves materials to do artwork are ways we can nourish our spirits and minister to ourselves.

Treat, however, is a loaded word, with connotations of pleasure that could also be harmful or not deserved. Treats are frequently used by abusers to lure children into accepting their attentions, thus becoming "tricks." We also have the verb *to treat*, "to deal with, to handle," and this can be done well or badly. Doctors and therapists *treat* their patients and clients, presumably to lead them towards health, although their methods may not always work and may not always be honourable.

If we are denied or deny ourselves genuine treats long enough, and are not treated well by others, we develop a kind

TREATS AND SECRETS

of "soul hunger," as Clarissa Pinkola Estes writes in *Women Who Run with the Wolves*. We may then try to snatch treats or express our creativity in secret, in small amounts or in binges. But secrecy, in creative pursuits as in love, can seriously distort our life force, our impulses and intuition.

This happens to the protagonist in Carol Shields's novel *Swann* when she hides her poems under the kitchen linoleum to keep them safe from her abusive husband. There is a fine line between safety and silence, protection and hiding.

When someone says, "This is a secret, don't tell anyone," the story becomes much more tempting to reveal. Secrets can be innocent ("We're giving Grandma a surprise party") or deadly and destructive. Like treats, secrets have many meanings. We can have a secret, private place where no one can intrude; or we can keep secrets about abuse, illness and family problems. In living, and in writing, we may gradually discover these secrets or find them revealed. Sometimes, in the telling, we realize that there was no need to keep them secret after all.

Secret places may, however, serve as safe places. In the novel *The Secret Garden* by Frances Hodgson Burnett, the garden becomes a healing place, a secret belonging to the three children until it can finally be revealed to the grownups. When Anne Frank began writing in her diary, she decided to give the diary a personal name, Kitty, as if she were talking to a friend, and she wrote,

> I hope I shall be able to confide in you completely, as I have never been able to do in anyone before, and I hope that you will be a great support and comfort to me.

Anne kept her diary while she and her family were in hiding in Amsterdam from the Nazis. It was her lifeline and provided her with a place to be safe from the dangers around her and to explore her feelings.

Diaries and journals through the ages have provided women with safe and private places to reveal their secrets and write about their lives. This in itself is a gift, a treat — often a lifeline.

Exercises

1. *Treats*

For this exercise, use the word "Treat" or "Treats" as your title, and do a timed writing of fifteen minutes. If it's hard to get started, you can try beginning with "I remember" or "I don't remember." For example, "I don't remember ever having treats at home, even on my birthday. My parents didn't believe in them. The only time my sister and I got treats was when we went to Mrs. Myers's house, down the road. She gave us ..."

You may want to do a simple list poem (described in the "Language" chapter) of all the real and well-loved treats in your life, past and present. These can include things like a sunny day, a phone call from an old friend, a backrub, as well as the "candy and flowers" kind of treat. You may want to consider treats you give and treats you receive.

2. *Someone Else's Secret*

This is an exercise to do in pairs or in groups. Each person writes down a secret, real or fictitious, and exchanges it with her partner or puts it in a hat for another group member to pick. Then you write a story about the other person's secret. This takes away some of the fears and inhibitions involved in telling secrets.

3. *Childhood Secrets*

If you are writing on your own, tell the story of a secret you kept from your parents or siblings when you were a child. This need not be a "deep dark secret inside your soul"; it could simply be a prank or exploit, or a private part of your life that you did not want anyone to know about at the time.

North

Winter
Earth
Wisdom, Remembering, Knowing
Completion, Gratitude, Silence
      and Readiness to Start again

> *Black clouds*
> *Swirling white lace*
> *I taste winter's first snowfall.*
>
>   — GINA SHELTON
>   "Seasons"

Solitude and Loneliness

> Alone, alone, all all alone
> alone on a wide wide sea ...
> — Samuel Taylor Coleridge,
> "The Ancient Mariner"

THERE IS A POINT in our journey when we need to enter a quiet inner space to reflect on where we're going, on current problems, or to give us time to heal and recover. This is often called solitude, which is meant to be a time we can give to ourselves — through writing, resting, listening to music, walking. Solitude can be crucial to the healing process.

Abusive and traumatic experiences are intrusive, breaking our personal boundaries and leaving us feeling invaded, even years later. As part of our healing, we may crave time alone, but then not know what to do with it when we have it. We may begin to feel anxious, prey to disturbing thoughts. We might criticize ourselves for wasting time and start performing tasks for others. We don't know how to let ourselves be alone with our thoughts and not be afraid of them. Instead we start to perform "useful" tasks like ironing or dusting. These routine tasks create a sense of pleasure and peace; they have a definite rhythm, a beginning and an end. Accomplishing them may help relieve depression and feelings of emptiness and helplessness; they may even give us satisfaction and fulfillment, but they may also prevent us from experiencing solitude.

North

Sometimes we need the feeling of drifting, of *not doing* anything useful or constructive, even of *not knowing* what we're going to do or what will happen. These times help us learn to be alone. Journalling can help you learn to be alone with yourself, to explore solitude, which is different from being lonely and allows you to be in *relationship with yourself*. It gives you time to get to know who you are, to get in touch with your feelings. By putting words on paper, you can work through the emotional clutter, even if this takes a little time getting used to. And if you are lonely, you can recognize that and find ways to make the feeling less oppressive.

Sometimes, if we are without a romantic partner or close friend, we feel we have failed at something, or think more about who or what is missing than what is there. Being lonely, however, may let us try something new — listening to music late at night and dancing around the living room, calling a new friend or taking a course. It's essential to resist the should's and can't's: I shouldn't go to a movie or play alone, I can't go on a trip by myself. At first, it's a hard step to take; but if you can do it once, you can do it again. You may even have fun and break through the "alone barrier." My great-grandmother, in the days when she was a young widow living with her daughter, son-in-law and grandchildren, used to go to the movies by herself when she got angry or upset. She would return in a happier state of mind, and family life would continue. Like my great-grandmother, you will come to value your time alone. You can use your journal to help you prepare for and reflect on these new experiences.

We sometimes become so busy with work, family and community obligations that we are starved for time alone but find it hard to say no to others, so we can take care of ourselves. One woman I know, Robin, remarked, "I feel like a peanut butter sandwich where the peanut butter is spread so thin on the bread that I don't get any." Finding an image like that for your need for solitude may help you get more of what you want.

SOLITUDE AND LONELINESS

Robin began making herself literal peanut butter sandwiches, not as a *substitute* for time alone, but to remind herself of her emotional as well as physical hungers and needs.

Another woman, Sarah, thought of her solitude as a medieval castle with fortified walls and a moat, whose drawbridge she let down occasionally. Inside was a thriving community, but it was fearful of invasion from outside. She learned that, in the Middle Ages, windows were developed only when people felt reasonably safe from attack. Sarah wanted to find ways of opening up some windows and doors in her castle, while still protecting her privacy.

The Jewish sage Hillel called for a balance between the poles of self and other: "If I am not for myself, who is for me; and being only for my own self, what am I?"

Solitude does not mean you are cutting people out of your life. It means setting boundaries that protect your right to time alone. And sometimes you need to step into your solitude to take care of yourself. Taking time out allows us to do this. Sometimes we also need to withdraw when we are in the company of others. We may feel uncomfortable in a given situation or we may be dealing with a momentary emotional experience. This may lead to miscommunication between you and someone else.

I was fortunate to be able to quickly resolve this kind of misunderstanding a few years ago. I have had, for some time, a fear of driving across certain bridges that seem particularly high or exposed. On my way to a summer writing workshop in New York State, I had to drive across a small bridge that, despite its size, precipitated a panic attack. I managed to get across the bridge and then pulled into the nearest service area to catch my breath. I heard a voice greet me in the parking lot: "Hi, Ellen!" It was a woman I had met and liked at the workshop the previous year. I mumbled a greeting and went in to get a coffee. It was only later that I realized I had been too preoccupied to be really friendly. I had withdrawn in order to deal with my panic.

That evening, when I saw her again at the workshop, I explained my state of mind when I'd met her at the service station.

My friend understood, and laughed in relief. "I thought you were mad at me," she said. "I wondered what I could have done over the winter to make you upset." We both smiled at the very human tendency to look at things from our own end of the telescope, and, in fact, the incident made us closer and better friends. After speaking to my friend, I was able to write a poem about the bridge, imagining the possibility of another route, and an alternative to panic. I could better understand the healing aspects both of that moment's solitude and of communicating the experience to a friend. So in my solitude I was not alone.

Exercises

1. *"I Wandered Lonely as a Cloud"*

This is a line by William Wordsworth. Write a dozen images of things or situations that are lonely. Your image can be as short as two or three words, or as long as two or three sentences. You can use personal situations ("as lonely as when I was a child in hospital, having my tonsils out") or images from the shared world around us.

2. *"I Want to Be Alone"*

This is Greta Garbo's famous line. Write two pages, or a timed writing of fifteen minutes, about a time when you really enjoyed being alone, either recently or when you were a child, or a time when you would like to be alone, now or in the near future.

3. *Two Solitudes*

Think of a time you have experienced a sense of solitude or aloneness with another person, either because of mixed signals,

SOLITUDE AND LONELINESS

like those described above, or because each of you was locked in your own separate place. Write about this from your point of view and then, if you can, from the other person's point of view. This may help create a bridge in your mind between the two solitudes, even if you are not able to speak directly to the other person.

❋

SILENCE

> If we had a keen vision and feeling of all ordinary human life, it would be like hearing the grass grow and the squirrel's heart beat, and we should die of that roar which lies on the other side of silence.
>
> — George Eliot, *Middlemarch*

Being Silenced

THERE IS A SILENCE that is nurturing, peaceful, that allows us to listen to deeper places in ourselves and in the world; then there is a silence that blocks speech, that denies and shuts out. This is the silence of not talking about the elephant in the living room, to use a popular metaphor; the elephant represents death, alcoholism, violence, abuse, any problem we don't want to see but which is taking up emotional space in our lives.

Listening to CBC's *Radio Noon* one day, I heard callers reacting to a call the previous day from a woman named Dorothy. She had phoned to say that if only women would be silent and know their place, wife abuse would not be a problem. She added that she herself had been abused, but learned to keep her mouth shut and now things were better. The callers mentioned how sad Dorothy sounded. Several said that women do need to speak out about abuse and that shelters and legal measures need to be out there to provide help.

Silence is one way to keep people trapped in an abusive situation. A woman afraid for her life, or her children's lives, may see silence as the only way to stay alive. Sometimes a woman

SILENCE

has to hide her voice inside to keep it intact, until she is *allowed* to express it *aloud*. Similarly, there is playwright Bertolt Brecht's story about a philosopher who was forced to work for the agent of a tyrannical regime, but never answered the agent's question, "Will you work for me?" After seven years of silence, the agent dies, and the philosopher gets rid of the body, cleans the house, and shouts "*No!*" Was this person a collaborator or a resister? Can we say for sure?

Thinking about Dorothy's phone call, I realized that, even though she advocated silence, she did this through a telephone call to a national radio station, hardly a silent medium. She was even able, on the phone, to disclose that she had been abused. There is a contradiction here which shows that, in truth, Dorothy is beginning to find her voice and take the first tentative steps towards using words to define her situation. Perhaps her words reached other women, also in abusive relationships who were sitting silently at their kitchen tables, *not* reaching for the telephone. Perhaps it helped them reflect on their own lives: "Should we be silent? *Is* that the right way?" Dorothy inspired people to call in, say their piece, reach out to her and show her that she is not alone.

Audre Lorde speaks clearly about the dangers of silence in her essay, "The Transformation of Silence into Language and Action":

> Death ... is the final silence. And that might be coming quickly, now, without regard for whether I had ever spoken what needed to be said, or had only betrayed myself into small silences, while I planned someday to speak, or waited for someone else's words ... I was going to die, if not sooner then later, whether or not I had ever spoken myself. My silences had not protected me. Your silence will not protect you. But for every real word spoken, for every attempt I had ever made to speak those truths for which I am still seeking, I had made contact with other women while we examined the words to fit a world in which we all believed, bridging our differences ...

North

And of course I am afraid, because the transformation of silence into language and action is an act of self-revelation. But my daughter ... said, "Tell them about how you're never really a whole person if you remain silent, because there's always that one little piece inside you that wants to be spoken out, and if you keep ignoring it, it gets madder and madder and hotter and hotter, and if you don't speak it out one day it will just up and punch you in the mouth from the inside." (*Sister Outsider*, pp. 41-42)

Women are taught to be silent and it's incredibly difficult for many of us to find our voice — often we write our voice first, before we learn to speak it out loud.

My friend Sandy James, a psychotherapist, normally has a strong voice and presence. A while ago she developed a bad case of laryngitis and had to write down what she wanted to say. "Without my voice, I feel I am invisible," she commented. It was as if not being heard reduced her power so much that she could not be seen, either.

This reminded me of the story of *The Little Mermaid*, especially the Hans Christian Anderson version I read as a child, not the prettified Disney version. The Little Mermaid gives up her voice — following the suggestion or demand of the sea witch — in order to gain legs. With legs she will be physically beautiful and "normal" and better able to attract the land prince with whom she has fallen in love. In the end, the prince rejects her and marries someone else. More accurately, he does not know of her love, since she cannot speak to him. She becomes lost to both worlds, land and sea. This story scared and saddened me as a child. As an adult, I realize that it exemplifies what happens to many of us as women — we give up our own voice, our power, our specialness, only to find we are not happy or do not belong in the world, or the relationship, for which we have become silent. Moreover, by this time we have lost the power to speak up to those around us.

The story made a particular impression on me as a child and adolescent because I was struggling with the issue of losing and finding my voice. My mother was a person who could literally lose her voice when she was upset. And there were definite unspoken taboos on talking about certain things (sexuality, bodily functions) and talking in certain ways in our home, although this lifted considerably as time passed on. I eventually wrote a poem about the little mermaid from the point of view of the sea witch, who was, in my mind, driven by "love" that was possessive but also tender.

In life, however, the story can have a better ending. We do not have to cast ourselves into the sea or silence ourselves permanently. We can learn to restore our voices, perhaps richer and deeper than before.

Many of us have reclaimed the ability to express the full range of our emotions, from grief and anger to joy, through voice. I had always been told, at home and at school, that I couldn't sing, that I should mouth the words. I was also told not to shout. At a vocal workshop with Canadian composer Wende Bartley, I began to sing notes consciously for the first time in my life. While singing a simple phrase ("Rising through the air") I began to have an image of shouting with joy. And my friend Judith, recovering from breast cancer, tells the story of another woman who said "Fuck you" to the doctor who had told her she had only a few months to live — and survived for years!

Monica L. Stevens lives on the Six Nations Reserve in Ohsweken, Ontario. Her poem "Silent Tears" may be for Monica herself (as a child and an adult) and also for the generations who are part of her history.

>SILENT TEARS
>They are so muffled and quiet
>But yet they are so very loud
>I am afraid someone will hear me
>"Shut-up, before I give you something to cry about"
>It hurts so much
>Please, let me scream!
>Hold me, and help me get it out.

North

> I'm older now.
> No one to tell me to shut-up
> My tears are silent
> Why can't I scream?
> It hurts so much
> Please, let me scream!
> Hold me, and help me get it out.
> — *Shaking the Rattle*, p. 3

We need women elders, relatives and friends who can help us. No matter what it takes or how we do it, we need to speak out, find and develop our own voices and ways of being.

Silence and Being

Sometimes, however, we are not *being* silenced but need to *be* in silence and turn off the noise and chatter around us and inside our own mind. We do this to discover what we really feel, or simply to live in the moment. This is the receptive, redemptive silence of watching the ocean or a campfire, or staring at a bird in flight. It might be the silence of meditation, or a quiet pause in a therapy session. One day, I was talking to a fourteen-year-old girl who was rattling on about her drama class and grade-eight graduation. She paused in her recitation, and instead of asking another question, I let the silence happen. After several moments she said, in a new, small voice, "My friend's baby sister died yesterday." The silence let her find the words to express what she was really feeling.

As I noted in talking about solitude, it is sometimes hard to be alone in the quiet of our own thoughts and feelings, especially in our fast-paced, noisy world. Sometimes we use words not to communicate but to provide a smoke-screen, so we don't have to listen to other people or to ourselves. But if you can allow yourself to be in this quiet state, you may find that new things to write about emerge from "the other side of silence,"

SILENCE

and come to enjoy the stillness at the center of yourself. In fact, two of the roots of the word silence mean "still or quietly flowing water" and "allowing (yourself) to be in a place." You might take a journal session to identify and write down all the noises, sounds and voices impinging on you during your day, and then turn off some of the background noises (e.g., television, radio) and see what happens.

Sometimes, too, it is the silence of being away from an absent friend or loved one that helps you discover your feelings about that person and find the words to express those feelings. Love letters and poems often come from this silence, this longing for someone who is not present.

When I ask students to find images for "quiet," they usually give thoughtful and moving responses. The first thing that comes to mind is "quiet as a mouse," but this cliché is so outworn that we no longer see a mouse, or hear the quiet. I point out, too, that mice are not so quiet — they squeak and scamper. What else can they think of? Almost always, the group begins to generate a long list of images showing a variety of situations and emotions, such as:

a forest after a storm
our house in early morning when everyone is sleeping
the silence in class just after someone has yelled
    at the teacher
a panther stalking its prey
a feather floating to the ground
a dust bunny
a child engrossed in building the perfect tower

Later, when I ask them to write about the quietest time they remember, they create haunting, deeply-felt pieces.

Another kind of silence, of course, is the profound silence of deafness, in which sound is not a factor in the world, and other senses may become more keen. I have seen plays performed by the Theatre of the Deaf that communicate powerfully to non-hearing and hearing alike, through gesture, movement and facial expression. There is an extensive Deaf culture that sees Deafness not as a disability but as an alternative to hearing culture. Writing by people who are Deaf helps them express their unique experience of the world and helps hearing people understand that experience.

If you are Deaf and beginning to write, you might use exercises 3 and 4 to write about a time with a particular emotional quality (e.g., peaceful, suspenseful, intimate), or about your experience of being Deaf. You may want to describe a particular experience in your life or reflect on your life as a whole.

EXERCISES

1. *Being Silenced*

Think of a time when you were silent but wanted to speak up on a certain issue, or to help another person. What held you back? What might have happened if you had spoken? Sometimes fear for your own life is a just and sufficient cause for silence.

2. *Speaking Out*

Is there a current issue that you want to speak up about? Write what you want to say. It could be a letter (to the person involved or a newspaper editor), a poem or simply a statement of your feelings and opinions. Or describe a time when you did speak up. What happened? How did you feel? Did you use words or gestures or other actions to make your point?

3. *As Quiet as ...*

Think of at least six images for quiet. These can be specific things like "The house was as quiet as a cemetery," or "After the storm, the air was quiet as a feather dropping." Or you could

SILENCE

use a metaphor like "The quiet was a lead weight," or "The silken quiet." Notice how you can use other senses, such as touch, to describe quiet.

Now, take one of these images and write more about it. Let the image open up and expand. Where does it take you? What do you hear? What do you see, smell, touch and taste? What emotion do you feel?

4. *The Quietest Time I Remember*

This can be a poem or a prose paragraph. You could try this exercise twice, once in your own voice, once in the voice of a person you know or the voice of a fictional character, an animal, or even an inanimate object (the telephone, the dining-room table). This kind of quiet happens in a setting, so describe this setting in detail. Does the quiet come at the end of the scene (e.g., a baby crying and finally sleeping), or at the beginning (e.g., the baby is sleeping, but then wakes up crying), or does it last throughout piece of writing?

You may find that the haiku and the bantu poetic forms, mentioned in the "Language" chapter, suit this exercise. In these forms, every word counts and the poem seems suspended in silence. You could write four haiku about quiet times or about quietness broken by a sudden noise, one for each season of the year. Or you can use the bantu form by thinking of one line with an image of silence or quietness. Then respond with a second line that contains another image:

> The telephone stopped ringing.
> Outside, new snow is falling.

You could use this form for writing about being silenced, too:

> I was too scared to say a word —
> The birds stopped singing.

DEATH

> There is a pain—so utter—
> It swallows substance up—
> Then covers the Abyss with Trance—
> So memory can step
> Around—across—upon it—
> As one within a Swoon —
> Goes safely—where an open eye—
> Would drop Him—Bone by Bone.
>
> — Emily Dickinson, *The Complete Poems*

I BEGAN WRITING this chapter on Halloween and continued on All Souls' Day, the day of the dead, an appropriate time to think and write about death. This is the time in many cultures when the veils between the worlds of life and death are said to be thin, and crossing between them is easier. It is also the time in the northern hemisphere when the earth itself is dying in order to prepare for a new spring: the harvest is in, plants are beginning to rest, leaves fall, bulbs are wintering underground.

Love and death are two of the most important subjects in writing and are often combined: we write about the death of a person or animal whom we loved. Sometimes when a relationship ends it feels like a death, and we need to grieve that loss too. This is a way of remembering and also a way to do something with our pain, our helplessness in the face of death or loss. Keening, mourning, wailing, chanting, singing prayers, writing

DEATH

poems — in a group or individually, aloud or silently — we invoke the spirits of the departed, shape their images, try to bring them back through imagination.

In Greek mythology, Orpheus was allowed to bring his dead love, Eurydice, back to life out of the underworld, as long as he did not look back at her on their return to earth. He disobeyed the taboo and lost her forever. Unlike Orpheus, we can learn to talk about the dead, knowing they are gone but bringing them once more into our lives. Even children can do this. For example, a nine-year-old boy in therapy makes a paper puppet representing his dead father: "John, meet Ellen. Ellen, meet John." An eleven-year-old girl in an enrichment class writes about her grandfather, who died when she was seven, "Some people say we never made the mobile we were planning, but I have a mobile of all our memories and experiences, hanging here inside my heart." These children found images as well as words to express their feelings.

Just as Mexicans and New Mexicans put marigolds and sugar candy on gravestones to feed and please the dead on the *Dio de los Muertos*, written words can also honour the dead and feed their memories and spirits. My mother used to tell me that people stay alive in memory, as long as we keep them in our minds and our hearts.

We think most often of single, individual deaths that can be mourned and remembered, of graves and cremation urns with individual names and identities. Death becomes much more overwhelming, even unthinkable, for people who have lost whole families and larger communities: Holocaust survivors; descendants of Africans brought to America in slave-ships and of Native peoples who died in forced marches, wars or resettlement; survivors of torture and of the "disappearances" in Latin America, or of massacres in Africa. Sometimes two or more generations must go by before someone can write about these events, when the grandchildren's desire to know about their origins can take precedence over the parents' desire to forget the tragedies and get on with survival.

The impetus to write about the death of someone close to you may come when you least expect it: in the midst of other activities, for example. Sometimes finding a metaphor that expresses your feelings about the death can make it easier to think about and to describe. On CBC Radio's *This Morning*, for example, Allan Wilson spoke about becoming immigrants to "the continent of Cancer" at the start of his son's (eventually fatal) illness, a journey to a harsh new land with its own language, customs and laws, separated forever from the "old country" of everyday life before the illness.

Your writing about death may take many forms; it might be a realistic account, a letter to the person who has died, a poem, a ghost story or a fantasy tale set in another world. Sometimes, in fantasy, we can make things happen that we know do not occur in everyday reality. In C.S. Lewis's *The Lion, the Witch, and the Wardrobe*, Aslan, the Lion, is killed because of "Deep Magic," but then, because of "Deeper Magic," death works backwards and he comes back to life. This children's novel may be read as a parable of Christ's death and resurrection; beyond any specific religious analogy, however, there is something powerful in itself about death going backwards. This reminds me of the scene in Kurt Vonnegut's *Slaughter-House Five*, in which a movie about the Second World War plays backwards so that bombs go back into the bomber bays in the planes, the planes go back to their hangars and, eventually, all the weapons of war are dismantled.

We "know" this cannot happen and yet, through miracle or imagination, it can. The fertility myths of the Corn King and Spring Queen, much older than Christianity, celebrate the dying and revival of nature. So do the Greek myth of Persephone's journey into the underworld and the Egyptian story of the descent into that realm by a woman named Inanna. Even the fairy tales of Snow White and Sleeping Beauty may have echoes of these earlier, powerful myths.

DEATH

Louise Da Salvo, author of *Writing as a Way of Healing*, says that there is no right way to write about death, and I agree. Find your own approach to deaths that affect you and write in your own time, whether this is immediately or in a while from now. You may need to write about the process of dying or you may prefer to focus on the life of the deceased person.

There is often a sense of guilt when someone dies. We feel, or say "if only ..." whether or not we had any way to avert death. We feel helpless in the face of death; we cannot turn it back, for other people or ourselves, much as we would like to.

During the inquiry into the contamination of the water supply in Walkerton, Ontario, I heard a woman talk about the death of her mother from the e-coli bacteria. She told the story to the judicial panel and to the public, to ensure that the kind of epidemic experienced in May 2000 would not befall other communities, other families. I also heard in her voice that telling the story, painful as it was, was healing. It allowed her to say goodbye, which she never had a chance to do during her mother's interrupted life. Inquests, inquiries, tribunals – they cannot bring the dead back to life, but they can help survivors find some meaning in experiences that are traumatic as well as grief-laden. If we think in terms of responsibility rather than blame, we have a better opportunity to correct faulty ways of doing things and thus make changes in the world.

We are sometimes moved to write about the death of someone we don't know well or have never met but have heard about through friends or through the news media. This is usually because something about the person or the circumstances of their death strikes a chord in our own lives, and because we feel the loss as part of our common humanity.

Sometimes there can be humour even in death, at a wake for example. This is partly, of course, to break the tension. Our reactions to death are often a surprise: we do not know what we will do, how we will feel, until it is happening.

Can we write about our own death? We may have had a

North

near-death experience of some kind, and come back changed, wanting to tell what we have seen. Or we may be entering "sacred space," the "other country" of the process of dying, and are writing about the physical, emotional and spiritual reality of this transition. We may be experiencing the death of a partner, family member or close friend. Sandra Butler, a feminist therapist, and her partner Barbara Rosenblum, a filmmaker, wrote *Cancer in Two Voices*, a journal they kept together and separately while Barbara was ill and dying. As well as writing about the illness and its effect on each of them, they wrote about the joy and pleasures they shared during these last few years, including their commitment ceremony. The final words about death and its aftermath were written by Sandra alone.

On the other hand, we may be quite well, but wondering about death, imagining how the world would go on without us or how we would go on without the world. I remember, as a child of five or six, wishing I could die to know what it felt like and where I would go, and then could come back to life to tell about it.

I have noticed that the theme of dead and dying children runs through my writing. Does this go back to my mother having a stillbirth when I was two-and-a-half, an experience I do not consciously remember? Is it linked to my own two miscarriages, when my son was a toddler? I'm sure these events influenced me, yet someone else might have lived through the same experiences and not needed to write about them, or written about them in a different way.

Here is one poem I wrote about the experience of miscarriage, about a year after it happened. Miscarriage and stillbirth is a silent, often unrecognized, death. A friend and colleague in England, Emmanuel Lewis, was one of the first people who encouraged parents to see, touch and name their stillborn children or late miscarriages; his work was helpful in enabling me to voice my own experiences, as I did in this poem:

DEATH

Wolf-Melody

Daughter-son
not-born a year ago
I think of you now
as I watch the sun slipping into Lake Huron
(or so it seems)
winking its one red eye.
Your brother, whom you will never know,
plays on the beach
making boats out of driftwood,
then acting out Brer Rabbit
playing dead to fool Brer Wolf, Brer Fox.
He does not really know what dead means,
Jumping up is part of the game.
He does not know he does not know you.
Named for my great-great-grandfather — and a song
bit of my body, my spirit — or your own
I have created you out of almost nothing
    memory of a sunset
    shadows in the night (hour of the wolf)
    expectancy of touching,
        laughter,
            tears
that I cannot yet
    let go.

Exercises

1. *Make a Will*

List not just your material possessions, but what legacy you want to leave to the world, to your community, to individuals —

what thoughts, gifts, understanding and wishes you would like to offer or grant.

2. "*A Woman Is Talking to Death*"

This is the title of one of Judy Grahn's most powerful and disturbing poems in her collection *The Work of a Common Woman*. If you could talk to Death, in any way at all, what would you say? Would you use any other means of communication in addition to, or instead of, words? Music? Dancing? Sex? Actions or activities, such as gardening or sports? How would you visualize Death in this conversation? What might Death say to you? What, in particular, could you say as a woman? You can write this as a story or a short play, written only in dialogue.

3. *The Empty Chair*

Think of someone who has died, and imagine that person sitting in a chair opposite to you. What would you like to say, and what might the person say? Imagine the dialogue, perhaps say it aloud, then write it down. Notice whether your thoughts and feelings change as you write.

A related exercise is writing a letter to someone who has died, a letter in which you are free to express all your feelings. After you write the letter, you might decide to keep it in a safe or special place, or you might decide to send it or let it go in some way — burning it ceremonially, tearing it into pieces and scattering the bits like ashes, burying it, even sending it up in the air in a helium balloon.

4. "*After the first death, there is no other.*" (Dylan Thomas)

What is the first death that made an impression on you? It might be a person, a pet, even a dead bird on the street. Write about it, letting associations come as they will.

❖

SPIRITUALITY

Magic. The world is full of magic. It's everywhere.
— Anne Cameron, "The World is Full of Magic,"
Celebrating Canadian Women

How do angels fly? They take themselves lightly.
— Anonymous

PRAYER, WORSHIP AND CONNECTION to the sacred comes in many forms, both in organized religions and in more individual or "alternative" beliefs. Many women have a deeply felt sense of personal spirituality within a framework of one of the major religions; other women are creating their own paths; for others, this is not an essential part of their lives. Any kind of spiritual connection may be a powerful inspiration for your writing. If spirituality is not a part of your life right now, you may wish to use this chapter to reflect on beliefs you have left or changed.

Many people are raised within one of the world's major religions: Judaism, Christianity in its various forms, Islam, Hinduism, Buddhism, Taoism, Shinto, and Native spirituality and practice. Some women continue to find sustenance in these traditions, while others may move from one religion to another. (Some Jewish women have become Buddhists, for example.) Sometimes, we leave and then return to the religion of our childhoods, as we get older or our lives change. A spiritual or personal crisis can make people lose their faith — or find it.

North

These religions approach the world and the idea of the divine differently and have had vastly different impacts on history and culture. Throughout history, we see the dichotomy between a constructive desire to seek and unite with the sacred, and the hierarchical power structures that lead to warfare, violence, hatred and repression. Some of us have experienced the oppression of power structures in a religious context. Writing about these hurts and how you've survived them can be healing. But what I would like to look at here are the positive aspects of spirituality in your own life, and the ways you can describe it in words and images.

All religions have sacred texts and stories, which are told over and over again, often as part of ceremonies. Some of the stories from the Bible have become part of common knowledge — stories like Adam's and Eve's creation and their temptation by the serpent, Noah's flood, the Virgin Birth and Crucifixion of Christ. Many of these stories probably evolved from earlier myths and stories, such as the Epic of Gilgamesh in Sumeria, which describes the flood, or Egyptian myths of the dying and rising god. Writers can work with these familiar stories in their own ways, making them personal and immediate. What did Eve really think about the serpent? How did the Magi feel on their long journey? Even giving a modern character a biblical name (e.g., Hagar Shipley in Margaret Laurence's *The Stone Angel*) sets up resonances and contrasts with the original story.

Writing can also come from your own meditations on religious symbols and ceremonies. I have written a children's story set during the Jewish holiday of Chanukah, with lighting candles in the menorah as the central image. In the following journal entry, Diane Goldsmith uses the imagery of Christian communion in a personal, intimate way:

> I wondered again this morning, have the birds always sung so sweetly? Or am I learning to listen in a new way? Senses open, I imagine taking the morning into me, a holy communion. Letting it slide down my throat and into my belly like rich red wine, strengthening my blood, my bones and my

SPIRITUALITY

passion for the day. The breath of morning air upon my skin, the touch of wind against my face, and the lingering aroma of honeysuckle warmed by the sun feed my morning hunger and nourish me for the day to come.
— Journal Excerpt, "Morning Musings," *We'Moon Calendar 2000*

This sensual description shows how spirituality can be felt with and through the human body, or the body of the earth. The metaphor of the Eucharist connects spirituality with nourishment. Perhaps this is a basic image for our experience of the divine — not outside us, but something we take into ourselves, that shakes us to new life and fills us with love. Union with the sacred is often expressed in erotic terms, too. Think of the Song of Solomon and of Hindu sculptures.

We often encounter the sacred in everyday activities, especially when we least expect it. Canadian modern dancer Margie Gillis, whose dancing is both spiritual and rooted in her body, has said that she would like the angels to come down and do dishes with her. On the other hand, we also connect to the spiritual by taking a break from everyday activities. Some people do this through organized religious services, or through meditating, drumming, chanting, lighting a candle, going on a vision quest or a silent retreat, or simply spending time in a place that feels special.

As in many other areas of life, women have been taking on more of a role in public as well as private spirituality. Mythology and religious stories and ceremonies from cultures around the world show, however, that women's spirituality has been a major force since earliest times, one that has never completely disappeared. Even if you are rooted in one tradition, it is enlightening to learn about goddesses and women spirit-figures from other cultures. In some of these beliefs, the woman creates the world, not by giving birth, but by her thoughts, her words, her songs. The Laguna-Pueblo people in New Mexico, for example, have the primal Thought Woman (sometimes called Old Spider Woman), who creates everything: "She is thought

North

itself, from which all else is born," says Paula Gunn in *The Sacred Hoop*. Many goddess figures are indwelling in the natural world — mountains and volcanoes, oceans, trees, the moon. In Iroquoian mythology, Sky Woman falls through a hole in the sky, and the turtle piles earth on its shell to make a place for her to land, thus forming "Turtle Island," or North America. The Hindu mother goddess Devi has many forms, including Parvati, the wife and mother whose animating power allows the god Shiva to create the world, and Kali, whose energy illuminates death and destruction.

Our own creativity may, on a personal level, reflect and reenact some of this deep, world-shaping power. Anne Lamott talks about images coming up from the "basement," or the subconscious. We have to be there to receive them and help them up. A friend of mine, an artist and teacher, believes that in the act of creating, energy bounces away from us, taps into a larger source and returns with new and greater energy, drawing in things we wouldn't have conceived of before. Katie Miller has written a book called *Holy Writ*, which explores various writers' ideas about the relationship between writing and religion. Can writing itself be seen as a kind of spiritual practice? Do we control our creativity, or are we inspired by something else? Maybe the questions are more important than the answers.

EXERCISES

1. *Special Moments*

In your present spiritual practice, is there an object, ceremony or holiday that you find particularly meaningful? This could be a traditional ceremony or celebration, or a private and personal one. If nothing suggests itself in the present, can you remember something from your childhood that had special

SPIRITUALITY

significance? Write for fifteen minutes about what this means to you. Include the experience of your senses, as well as your thoughts and feelings.

2. *Praying and ...*

There is a Zen Buddhist story in which the master tells his disciples that you cannot smoke while you pray, but it is all right to pray while you smoke. Describe an activity *not* related to a religious service, in which you feel prayerful. Begin with the verb or verb-phrase naming that activity, for example,

    e.g., Canoeing ...
    When I wash the dishes ...

You can add the word "sometimes," as in "Sometimes when I'm washing the dishes, I ..."

Or "Sometimes, canoeing alone across the lake, I ..."

3. *Retelling the story*

Think of a biblical or sacred story and tell your own version of it. Perhaps you want to take the point of view of a character who is present but does not have a major role in the traditional telling of the story. Or perhaps you have other ideas of how the story might have really happened. You can be human or animal, even vegetable or mineral (the Tree of Knowledge, for instance, or the Red Sea), or a spiritual being.

4. *Now I lay me ...*

Going to sleep and first waking are times of change from one state to another. At these times we are more open to prayer, reverie and communication with spirit. Many of us grew up with this prayer:

> Now I lay me down to sleep
> I pray the lord my soul to keep
> If I should die before I wake
> I pray the lord my soul to take

North

It is written in rhyming couplets: the first line rhymes with the second; the third line rhymes with the fourth. The rhyme helps us remember the intention. Whatever your feelings about this particular prayer, write your own four-line prayer in two rhyming couplets that you would like to say at bedtime or when you get up in the morning. It could be for yourself, for someone close to you, like a child or other family member, or for the world at large.

❋

The Circle of Time

We are accustomed to visualizing time in a straight line. But perhaps our time-lines are as limited as flat maps. On a map, the four directions appear at opposite sides, seemingly never to meet; yet on a globe we can see east become west, north become south. Maybe the aspects of time also interconnect in ways of which we are not fully aware.

For the purposes of this book, we will talk about past, present and future as distinct directions, but allow that there are back-and-forth connections between them, and that, as in the children's saying, "yesterday's tomorrow is today, and will become yesterday tomorrow."

Past

> It's the stories that last, across borders and time.
> — Michele Landsberg

Grandmothers, Mothers and Other Wise Women

MENTION "GRANDMOTHER" to almost anyone, and you'll get a story, oral or written. In fact, writing about their grandmothers seems to be the impetus for many women to begin writing. You can begin with a name and a picture. Mary TallMountain, a poet with Athabascan as well as Scottish-Irish heritage, wrote about her grandmother, Matmiya, whose name means "mountain," using the image of a mountain, deeply connected to the earth. (Cited in Bill Moyers, *The Language of Life*)

In *Intricate Countries*, I have written poems about both my great-grandmother and my grandmother, using images of growing plants. The one about Mary, my great-grandmother, is called "Roots":

> I see you stand in your warm kitchen
> growing sweet potatoes in jam jars ...
> I cannot remember your voice,
> only your eyes, smiling at me from old photographs
> and the oven of my dreams.

One of her daughters became my grandmother, and when I wrote "For Rose Albert" I used her name as the central image:

The Circle of Time

> Rose, bloom of my childhood,
> Grandmother ...
> I remember
> your rose-painted nails
> and nestling in your feathery bed
> when I slept over.

It was much later that I read Natalie Goldberg's *Writing Down the Bones* and found her suggestion to begin a piece with "I Remember" and also "I Don't Remember," both of which I had done in these poems.

How do we know what we don't remember? Maybe we have heard family stories or legends, maybe we know the questions and not the answers, maybe there are things we, or our families, have not wanted to remember. Keep in mind, too, that personal memory is not like a tape recorder or video camera. Inevitably, no two people remember an event in the same way, and the same person may remember an event in different ways, at different times in her life. There is no "one truth," but many truths coming together.

Grandmothers are often links to another culture, to our roots. In the anthology *Our Grandmothers, Ourselves: Reflections of Canadian Women*, edited by Gina Valle, eighteen women from seventeen different cultural backgrounds reminisce about their grandmothers and how they influenced their childhoods and their present lives. One of the women, Alys Murphy, says that "Writing about my grandmother consolidated my understanding of the heroism of ordinary women's lives." They bring us in touch with other languages, other foods, other music (even if they try to become "Canadian."). Eva Tihanyi's memoir notes that "We all come from somewhere, and it is important to understand what that 'somewhere' entails." By looking at all the cultures and histories that make up our lives, we understand ourselves better as individuals, and as Canadians.

Hearing your grandparents' language, even if you don't understand all the words, can give a sense of comfort and also

PAST

a sense of belonging to another world, another home. It can be the voice of story and song, of lullaby, of prayer, of holidays and ceremonies, of secret grownup talk, perhaps even of swearing. Using the language of your grandmothers in writing can also help you think in different ways, as we have noted in "Language."

Richard Douglass Chin, a Hamilton writer who was born in Trinidad, with African and Chinese grandparents, used some Yoruba (a West African language) in a long poem about his grandmother on market day. The mixing of English and Yoruba gives us the feeling of the grandmother's world, especially as seen by a small child clinging to her skirts, as we see in this excerpt. Notice the play of rhymes in English as well as the Yoruba phrases, both of which give the poem a songlike flavour.

MARKET DAY

Iya agba e wa. Iya agba e wa.
E wa, e wa, e wa. Iya agba e wa.
Come, Grandmother, come.
It is market day.
Ojo oja l'oni
Let us go down the way together
E je k'ajo lo
E je k'ajo lo si ilu
Let us go down together to town
the weather rainy
Ojo nro
Rain is falling
calling you and I
E yin ati emi
Labe ofurufu dudu
Under blue-grey sky
In the sultry heat of the afternoon
Ninu ooru osan gangan
In the sweating heat of the high afternoon
So sweet in June is Charlotte Street ...

The Circle of Time

Relationships with mothers are often more ambivalent than those with grandmothers, including both closeness and distance, love and anger. As we get older, and perhaps become mothers ourselves, we may begin to look at the past in a new way, and see things from our mother's or grandmother's point of view as well as our own. In "Burn Sugar" by Marlene Nourbese Phillips, the narrator is making a black sugar cake. She remembers helping her mother make the cake when she was a child, and phones her to ask for directions. As she stirs, she is thinking of what the cake means; the burnt sugar, turning the batter shades of brown from light to dark, makes her think of her family and other African people taken from their homeland on slave-ships to Canada and the United States. Her mother tells her the cake is "just a cake," meant to be eaten. But the narrator disagrees: "everything has a meaning," she says. In the end, we wonder if they are both right.

We learn many things from our mothers, some taught by direct instruction, some by example. Sometimes we say to ourselves, "I'll never do *that* the way my mother did," and years later, find ourselves doing just that. Or knowing, suddenly, *why* she did that.

Similarly, becoming a grandmother brings about many changes: you may remember your grandmother in a new way, and you may form a relationship with your grandchildren that is loving but (usually) not the same as the relationship with your own children. There are also changes in your relationships with the parents of your grandchildren. In addition, you become aware of growing older and of the continuity of generations — another way of looking at the circle of time.

Other women relatives are also important in our lives. Many of us had a maiden aunt, a woman who did not marry but worked and travelled, at a time when not many women did these things independently. My great-aunt Zelda, a nursery school teacher, took me to the theatre, out for lunch and on occasional trips, treating me more like an equal than did my mother or grandmother. One of my regrets is not going with her to Mexico, where she spent many vacations and made good friends. Many of these aunts valued women's friendship and showed us that was important.

Grandmothers and mothers do not have to be women in our immediate families. We can meet quite a few wise women during the course of our lives, if we are open to this experience. Jacqueline Lawrence, an Ottawa poet, has written about "My Five Moms" in her community. Going swimming at the Y in the early mornings, I have met two women in their seventies to whom I feel close. Becoming aware of older women's lives helps us age with dignity and compassion. This is especially true in mainstream society which glorifies youth and does not usually regard older people as Elders.

Many women have not had the experience of growing up with a mother. Their mothers may have died or abandoned them. These can be especially difficult experiences. Their mother isn't there to guide them through adolescence and young adulthood, and the daughter may miss her mother at crucial times in her own life. Hope Edelman's *Motherless Daughters* and Helen Vozenilek's *Loss of the Ground Note: Women Writing about the Loss of their Mothers* focus on the many issues of motherloss and how women write, speak and recover.

I have not talked about women's relationships with fathers, grandfathers, brothers and other important male figures. Male relatives and mentors can also shape our lives in a variety of ways, both positive and negative. As women, we may need to work on dealing with the relationships with men in our lives, as well as with women, to find our own wholeness. Writing can help us acknowledge the strengths and the wounds of these relationships, as well as find some healing.

I have written several pieces about my father, a cardiologist who loved baseball and jazz, especially concerning his illness and death and also a time he was away from home for several months when I was young. I feel that I am, metaphorically, in

The Circle of Time

the business of being a "heart doctor," creating a bond between us. Other women have had difficult, painful experiences with fathers and father figures who were abusive or absent. The exercises below can be adapted to writing about fathers, and you can draw on your own memories and experiences in writing other pieces about them.

Heirlooms and Hand-Me-Downs

In a column in the *Toronto Star*, Michele Landsberg wrote about a samovar, a family heirloom that an uncle was bringing to her house. She had many memories of this samovar, memories especially strong and sweet, like Russian tea, because they were connected to her parents, grandparents and other relatives. Even though the uncle finally decided he could not part with the samovar, she said that was all right because it is the stories, the memories, that really matter and need to be cherished. Phoebe Gilman has adapted an old legend into a children's story on this theme. *Something from Nothing* is about a baby blanket that becomes a jacket, a vest, a tie, a handkerchief, a button — and finally, when gone, a wonderful story.

Many of us have items, or memories of items, handed down through our family. These may be treasures or things we would rather do without, but they all tell a story. When my writing group chose the topic of hand-me-downs, we produced some deeply felt writing.

My hand-me-downs include a black cashmere sweater that my grandmother Rose received for her ninety-first birthday. All her life she had enjoyed dressing well, and at that age, she still lived alone in her own apartment, healthy except for a bit of osteoporosis, and clear in her mind. She died two years later, still living capably on her own, and when my mother and I cleaned up her things, my mother suggested that I take the sweater. For a over a year it sat in my drawer; I could not wear it. Then, one cold November day, it seemed natural to slip it over my head. I thought I could still smell her scent. Now —

PAST

years later — I still wear it, the sleeves frayed and mended. I've also been given a tweed jacket owned by the deceased mother of a close friend of mine; when I wear it, I feel held in the love that my friend and her mother shared.

What do we keep and what do we throw out? I have been grappling with this question lately, as I moved to a new city and my son left home for university and then work. This common household dilemma represents one of the processes of life: keeping space clear for moving on while holding on to those things that keep the past alive for us.

Material things are fragile, subject to loss, breakage and decay. My father-in-law played the trombone as a young man in Saskatchewan, and also in the Canadian Navy during the Second World War. All his records warped while they were stored in a basement. I was sorry not to have heard them, but he still can hear the music in his head, and we know that he played this music and enjoyed it. Family photographs are another good way of keeping in touch with the past — although they often raise questions, which no one may be alive to answer.

For people whose families have lived through genocide or massive catastrophe of any form, these losses are much harder and more extreme. People, places and things are annihilated, and the survivors often do not want to talk about their memories — "even the happy times," remarked a woman I know, whose parents lost close relatives in the Nazi concentration camps. Sometimes, as mentioned earlier, it takes two or three generations before a family can even begin to talk about these aspects of their past.

The Circle of Time

EXERCISES

1. Flower or Mountain

Think about one of your grandmothers, and find a metaphor or image to describe her. Use it in a prose memoir or a poem. Stretch the image and see where it takes you. You might want to start your piece with "I remember" or "I don't remember."

You can also write about an older woman you know and admire, or about your grandfather.

2. "A Piece of Advice"

In Dayal Kaur Khalsa's *Tales of a Gambling Grandma*, the grandmother gives her granddaughter "a little piece of advice" and some "laws of life." For example: "Draw people with red cheeks so they look happy. Boys play with guns, girls play with dolls." (This comment leads to interesting discussions when I read the book to children.) What, if any, advice did your grandmother, or any older relative, give you? Do you follow it? Why do you think this was important to her? Think about the difference between advice that someone teaches or tells you, and the things you learn from example and observation.

3. The Worth of One Picture

If possible, find a photograph of your grandmother at any point in her life. What does the picture tell you? What would she say if she could speak? Write a monologue, about a page long, as if your grandmother were speaking or thinking out loud. She could be the age that she is in the photograph or she could be older, looking back at herself at that time and place.

If you have many pictures, you might want to put together a collage to accompany your writing. And if you have no pictures, you could try drawing one yourself. Or you could look for a photograph of a woman who suggests some characteristics of your grandmother.

4. Heirloom

Tell the story of an object or heirloom you have, or one that you know about from family stories. You can tell the story of the first person who owned or used this object — if you don't know all the details, make them up. Or do a bit of research, asking other family members, if you can.

Instead, or in addition, tell the story from the object's point of view: "I am a gold brooch ... a tweed jacket ... a trombone ..." Describe what has happened to you over the years, and how it felt. Have you liked your life, or not? What do you hope for now?

Future

I learn by going where I need to go.
— Theodore Roethke, "The Waking"

As children, most of us enjoyed surprises. Some of us are temperamentally wired to need more routine and structure in our lives, with adequate time to prepare for transitions, while other people can more easily go with the flow. If we have had too many sudden, abrupt, and unpleasant shocks and changes in our lives, we may need a more orderly life — or, on the other hand, we may construct a life of high drama and turbulent roller coaster rides, such as addictions of one kind or another, or sudden changes in jobs, partners, homes.

Someone has said that "the only constant is change." I think that we need both order and surprise in our lives. We need structure and long-term commitments to feel safe. But we need surprises to keep life interesting. Besides, surprises and changes come whether we want them or not.

My son used to watch a television show called *Masters of the Universe*. In one episode of this show, the oldest, largest tree in the forest agrees to be cut down so that evil will not take over the planet. Several forest creatures beg the tree to reconsider. "If you're cut down, things won't be the same," they moan. "Well, then," says the tree in a deep voice, "they will be *different*." That line has stayed with me, and has been a great help in times of change.

FUTURE

Our fear, I think, is that the known world will be gone — *Poof! Disappeared!* — when there is a major change. There will be a cartoonlike black hole in the centre of our universe, and it certainly won't be funny. More often, the truth is that we do go on, but things are different. Images from science, like black holes in space, time warps, red and blue shifts, are useful in conveying the shock to our physical world that change often involves, as if the laws of physics themselves are being overturned by unknown forces.

Mary Catherine Bateson's book *Composing a Life*, based on the stories of five professional women including herself, shows us the importance of *improvisation*. We start from something known, but then play with it, ad lib, whether it's a recipe, a trip across country or a writing project. Writing can help us notice and adjust to the surprises in life, and use them in more creative ways. Your journal can accompany you through inconsistencies, different points of view, various ways of looking at yourself and the world. Like a snake shedding its skin, we sometimes need to change even things that were once dear and indispensable to us.

We can also use the element of surprise in our writing, I remember hearing a Canadian poem about a "white horse leaping into the perfume department at Eaton's." I do not remember the author, but that image has stayed in my mind. I could see the white horse, elegant but full of energy, disrupting the neatly arranged perfume counter and the fashion-magazine idea of beauty and decorum. Sometimes we want our writing to be "nice," as we learned in school. When a poem or story seems to need something, I realize it may be time for the white horse to gallop in. In other words, I need to find an image, a character, an action, a "people-startling word" to enliven and deepen the piece. When we are open to this kind of awareness, we let in new words, rhythms, voices, things we didn't know we knew. It's exciting to hear a character shouting in your ear, "Listen! This is what I have to say."

The Circle of Time

On the other hand, poetry makes use of structure, such as repetition, rhythm, rhyme and line count, and prose has its own forms and conventions. These give writer and reader some guidelines, containing the material so we do not become lost or overwhelmed. Experimental art breaks out of old forms and creates new ones — until they, in their turn, become traditional and new artists come along to develop new forms. In your own work, it is important to find the balance that feels right for you.

Surprises in life may give rise to creative inspiration. This happened in the life of novelist Margaret Laurence, when she was living in Oxfordshire, England, in the late 1960s. A colony of moles invaded Laurence's front lawn, digging tunnels, making molehills and generally disrupting the grounds of her rented home. She called the exterminator; by the time he came, a few days later, she had started a novel for young people, *Jason's Quest*, about a mole who goes on a quest to save his city from a mysterious illness. He meets other animals, faces dangers and his own fears, falls in love, and finally discovers — just in time — that the illness is *boredom and fear of change*.

This is a wonderful metaphor for creative thinking and living. Instead of turning the molehill into a mountain of annoyance, Laurence transformed it into a book. I'm sure that many of the themes were already in her mind, but the unexpected moles on her lawn served as a creative spark. Discovering the novel also directly changed my life. Captivated by the story and characters, I requested permission from Laurence's estate to adapt it into a play for children, which received its first production in 2001.

Sometimes when you feel stuck in the present, it helps to write a letter to yourself from the future, imagining that you have achieved one or more of your goals, or that you are over the rough spot in your life. You can congratulate yourself for getting there and review the steps you took.

By making the future exist in the present, you may find you know how to get there. Although you don't know for sure what

FUTURE

will happen, by changing the perspective in time, you can see things differently and develop new confidence, even envision new possibilities. It's like entering a time warp. To use a different image, it's like reading ahead in a book that you yourself are writing. My friend Mickie Grover and I once talked about moving into "Chapter 13" — the next chapter in your own life. Some people suggest living as if you were going to live forever; other people, as if you have only one day or one month left. We don't know what life holds for us, but we know it is important to live with hope.

EXERCISES

1. *Surprise Encounters*

Remember an enjoyable and surprising discovery you made while travelling or even in your own neighbourhood. It need not be monumental; usually, it is the small, out-of-the-way things that mean the most. Sometimes it's as simple as seeing a snowman that someone built at one of the busiest intersections, or a conversation with a stranger on a train. You could write this in the form of a letter describing the experience to someone else.

2. *Mental Notes*

As you move through your days, note and observe when you follow routines and when you step off the beaten track, do something on the spur of the moment, or follow a hunch. Don't judge yourself, but keep an eye out for those situations and see what happens.

The Circle of Time

3. Following White Horses

As you read, note things writers do that surprise you: characters, plot devices, imagery, ways of structuring the work. Does this help the story, essay or poem, or hinder it in some way? Could you adapt any of these techniques for your own writing?

4. Letter to Yourself from the Future

For this exercise, choose a particular part of your life where you feel stalled, stuck or without direction. Perhaps you have some idea where you'd like to go, perhaps not. Imagine that it is five, ten, even twenty years later than it is right now. Write for fifteen minutes, at least two pages, about where you are and what you are doing. Be as specific as you can. You can focus on the problem you began with, but you may discover other parts of your life that have changed too.

When you've finished, read your letter over, then put it away in a safe place. In a week or so, read it again. Does it suggest anything you might need to be doing now? Either way, put it back in the safe place, and refer to it at intervals, especially when the time period is up. You may want to do this exercise with a friend or partner, each of you keeping a copy of the other's letter as well as your own.

❊

Present

> Yesterday is history
> Tomorrow is mystery
> Today is a gift —
> That's why it's called the present.
> — *Anonymous*

I CLOSE the Circle of Time with the present because this is where we are, *here* and *now*. These guidelines can help us stay present, in each moment:

Show up

Pay attention

Tell the truth

Don't worry about the outcome

These are good to keep in mind for your writing, and for other situations as well.

In this chapter, I would like to focus on friends, people who are present for each other in the now. You may have a few close friends and then a wider circle of friends, some of whom met each other through you. Some friendships form through work or leisure activities, like sports teams or choirs; some go back to childhood or college days, enduring over time and distance. Friendships may grow and deepen with time, or wear thin, or end in anger; sometimes they can grow close again.

Sometimes friendships arise through circumstance. In the 1990 film *The Company of Strangers*, a group of elderly women are thrown together when their tour bus breaks down near an old house in rural Quebec. Wary at first, they begin to exchange confidences and become friends. The cast were not professional actors, but hired to play themselves. Mary Meigs, a painter and writer who appeared in the film, has written that the lives of all the women were changed by the filming and several have remained real-life friends

Deeper than talking and doing things together, there is a level of comfort and safety and being known that you feel with a good friend, of any gender. As Elbert Hubbard put it, "A friend is someone who knows all about you and still likes you."

Sometimes people can be friends and lovers at the same time. The character Sixto, in Toni Morrison's *Beloved*, says of the Thirty-Mile Woman,

> She is a friend of my mind. The pieces I am, she gather them and give them back to me in all the right order. It's good, you know, to have a woman who is a friend of your mind. (*Beloved*, p. 335)

Liking someone as a friend may be a low-level attraction, not the intense chemistry of a romantic relationship. Sometimes we fall in love with someone who has been a friend, and some people find that it's possible to be friends with ex-lovers, now that you're on the far side of intimacy. Other people sever all connections after a breakup. Sometimes, divorced parents may actually become friends as they stay in contact to deal with their children.

Schoolchildren often have "best friendships" that have some of the storminess of romance, perhaps because they don't yet have romantic relationships. "Jessica isn't my friend any more," Amanda tearfully exclaims. Two days later, they are best friends again.

If we are estranged from family, or simply living far away, friends can become like family. And old friends carry each other's memories, reminding each other of times past, supplying details the other person has forgotten. Friends can also help you see things from a new perspective, without judging you, and they can help you shake old habits and defences.

PRESENT

We say "just friends," as if friends were not just as important, in a different way, as the other people in our lives. Friends are people we can play and have fun with — whether that means going to a movie or a baseball game, talking about relativity or simply having a cup of tea together. Sharing experiences and having fun together can replenish you, make you feel happier and sometimes stir the pot of ideas for writing.

Friends are people you can say no to, without fear of recrimination. "No, I'm sorry, I'd like to see you but I need this time to do something else." On the other hand, sometimes a friend suggests doing something you'd never have thought of by yourself. You go ahead and do it together, and have more fun than you expected.

In troubled times, writing is one ally, and the company of friends is another. My friend Judith recently held a gathering to celebrate the one-year anniversary of her surgery for breast cancer. She made it through chemotherapy and radiation, and is now cancer free and feeling well. Several friends had helped her through this ordeal, and now she wanted us all to come together with good food and wine and conversation, acknowledging and releasing the stress of the past year.

How can friends directly affect your writing? We've looked at "cheerleaders for your writing" in "Barriers and Pathfinders to Writing," but you can also have one or two friends who can be writing buddies, people with whom you make a date to write together, each of you working on your own piece, then reading aloud. Writing groups are another way to work with friends. I will talk about them in the concluding chapter.

We can also have friends *in* books. There are books we return to again and again, like old friends, and certain characters whom we get to know and continue to think about when we put the book down. When I read C.S. Lewis's *Narnia* stories to my son (I'd missed them in my own childhood), I often wanted to meet Aslan, the Lion, and have him give me some advice. And more recently, I've thought I would like to have lunch with the characters in Jane Rule's *Memory Board*. Other characters are not necessarily people you would like as friends, but they continue to live in your imagination. And Diane Goldsmith, quoted earlier, says that her journal itself is "like an old, familiar friend."

In *A Room of One's Own*, Virginia Woolf remarks on how surprised she was to find the words "Chloe liked Olivia" in a modern novel. In older literature, she had rarely seen women represented as *friends*: they were usually shown in their relationships to men. Woolf felt that novels could now begin to show women as independent adults, capable of developing personal and working relationships with each other.

Women's friendship has become much more important in novels over the years. For example, Doris Lessing's *The Golden Notebook*, which I devoured during my last year of university, has the friendship between Anna and Molly at its core. Lynn Kanter's *On Lill Street* and *The Mayor of Heaven* deal with friendships among both lesbian and heterosexual women, and between women and men. "It isn't often that someone comes along who is a true friend and a good writer. Charlotte was both," wrote E.B. White in *Charlotte's Web*. What a goal to aim for!

EXERCISES

1. *Circles of Friends*

Draw several rings of concentric circles, like ripples in a pond, with yourself at the centre. Place your closest friends in the circle nearest you and work out from there. If no one is really close, you may want to start in the second or third circle. You may need to show how some friends can be close and far away at the same time. You may rarely see someone who lives far

PRESENT

away, yet feel an emotional bond. Conversely, your nextdoor neighbour may be quite friendly, but you just don't feel the connection of true friendship, "kindred spirits" in Anne of Green Gable's words. Use this map to think about the patterns of your friendships. Is there anything you'd like to change?

2. *Around the Kitchen Table*

This is a place where friends often gather. Write a piece with this title, as a timed writing (fifteen to twenty minutes, or about two to three pages).

3. *A Literary Tea Party*

Plan a lunch, tea or dinner party for a group of your favourite authors or characters, past and present. Choose, say, half a dozen individuals. Whom will you invite? How will they get along? What will you serve? Write the answers to these questions, and then a short dialogue or encounter between two or three of these people.

4. *The Present Tense*

Writing in the present tense (I walk, she says) gives an immediacy and vitality to your writing, while the past tense gives more opportunity for reflection. Write a paragraph about an everyday incident in the present tense, then in the past tense, and notice the differences.

❉

Opening Doors

Women will draw doors where there are none, and open them and pass through into new ways and new lives.

— CLARISSA PINKOLA ESTES,
Women Who Run with the Wolves

"EVERYTHING ELSE"

WHEN MY SON WAS YOUNG, he had a book called *Grover and the Everything in the Whole Wide World Museum*, in which the Sesame Street character goes on a field trip through a museum, looking at everything from dinosaurs to postage stamps, portraits to musical instruments. Finally, he sees a door marked "Everything Else." He proceeds happily through the door, only to find himself in the wide world outside the museum, with trees, houses, people, weather, a huge sky overhead. This is the limitless world of experience, more wonderful than the exhibits in the museum.

This door marked "Everything Else" is the final door of this book. You can write about anything. Your experience, vision and life's journey can encompass anything and everything. This door is Spider Woman spinning her web out of her own essence. It is an Open Sesame to creativity. We have come full circle, and you are ready to begin again. This book has given you some of the tools and ideas that you will need. You will make, or find, others along the way. You are ready to open, or create, the last door — the end that is, in fact, the beginning.

And if you think you have picked the wrong door, go back and try again — or look around a bit before you decide. Remember that "Everything Else" is infinite, and most of it is yet undiscovered, unnamed, unreported.

Although in this book we have focused on several specific topics, the best advice for being open to your writing and your inner self comes from Marion Milner's book, *A Life of One's Own*, in which she talks about paying attention to your thoughts as they arise, not as if they are heavy burdens or responsibilities, but as if they are butterflies whose swirling paths you can follow. Often, we have to consciously allow ourselves to slip into the mode of reverie, of noticing and accepting. Just as sometimes we can remember a name when we let ourselves forget about it (letting our unconscious mind do the work), so in writing, we need to look out of the corner of our eye, follow our attention along the snags of detail, colour, sound, smell, emotion, resemblance, even if we are not sure where they will lead.

Here are some practical ways to continue with your writing life.

Connecting with Others

If you are not a member of a writing group, you might want to think about joining one or forming one of your own. Places to ask for information about writing groups:

- Women's bookstores, or any good independent bookstore
- Public libraries
- Universities, colleges, or community education centres
- The YMCA/YWCA
- Seniors' centres
- Reading groups or other clubs to which you belong

Women's bookstores are particularly good places to find a writing community, as well as interesting books. Especially in this time of large chain emporiums, it is important to support independent bookstores. Women's bookstores, such as The Toronto Women's Bookstore or A Women's Place Bookstore in Calgary, often take an active role in the community, offer workshops in writing or the arts, sponsor readings and concerts, and may become involved with politics, social justice and environmental activities.

If you can't find a group, you can create one. Think about what kind of group you'd like: a small, stable group limited to people you know, or a more open one. The former are more likely to develop intimate writing relationships; but strangers and new people can bring their own stimulation. If you want a closed, invitational group, find a few friends who are interested in meeting regularly to write together (e.g., weekly, every other week, monthly). If you are already a member of a book club or similar group, see if some of those people would like to form a writing group. If you want an open group, you can also put up notices at bookstores, libraries, and other places mentioned above. Decide whether you want to limit your group to women, or if you want to work with women and men. Either can work well, depending on the people involved. You may also decide to turn your open group into a closed group when you find a combination of people who work well together. And closed groups can decide to include new members on occasion, enriching and enlivening the mix.

You can ask a local writer to help you get started, but I don't think writing groups need a leader. Instead, members of the group need to agree on a basic format. The Women's Work Writing Workshop in Hamilton that I have been working with for several years meets every second Thursday. This seems to be about the right interval for us; most of us work and have family responsibilities, as well as other meetings to go to, so weekly would be too often, while monthly would seem too long a gap. Members are free to miss a meeting if necessary, or even to take a sabbatical from the group and return. We do not have any official membership structure.

We usually meet at one woman's home, around her kitchen table. Tea, water and other drinks are available; sometimes women bring snacks to share. At the end of each meeting, we decide on a topic for the next session, work on it at home and read our pieces aloud at the next meeting. But we are easy about rules; a woman may write on something else entirely, or choose not to write that week. After sharing our work, we select another subject for a timed writing of ten or fifteen minutes, and then read that aloud to the group. The combination of writing

Opening Doors

at home and also writing while we are together seems to work well.

Sometimes we exchange news of contests, readings and books. Gradually, we learn more about each other's lives. For the last several years, the group has held a public reading open to all women in the community, the May Muse. And for the last two years, we have gone on weekend retreats together. Several women have found that their work shapes itself into a longer project during this extended time; as we eat and live together, our energies deepen and focus.

Each group, however, needs to work out its own way of doing things, and discuss what is effective and what may need to change. The important thing is that the people who come feel safe and in tune with each other, so that each person is free to offer her story, knowing that she will be heard and respected. Sometimes the group hears wonderful things in a piece of writing that the author hasn't seen; sometimes they can offer suggestions, in the spirit of the writing, that push the piece further. The support of a group makes it easier to sit down in front of the blank page, to do the "assignments" and develop our own ideas.

You can also go to writing retreats or workshops that meet yearly for a week or two (usually in the summer), in some more faraway place. You can go back to the same centre year after year, meeting new people and deepening the connections with other regulars. On the other hand, you can sample many different workshops in different places. There are ones for women and for women and men together, and for specific cultural groups. The U.S magazine *Poets & Writers* has a good list of workshops in various parts of the U.S.; Canadian workshops can often be found by looking through literary magazines such as *Grain* and *The Fiddlehead*.

For more experienced writers and other artists, there are also centres where you can go for a month or more to work on a specific project. These have a more formal application procedure; they can be expensive, but many provide some financial assistance.

Forming a writing group on the Internet is another possibility. For people living in remote locations, for writing friends who live far apart or for people with special needs or conditions that make meeting in person impossible, e-mail can be a welcome connection. There are also electronic writer mentoring programs, where writers and students communicate online.

There are many Web sites offering information about writers and writing across Canada, and the world. There are so many, so often changing, that it is impossible to list them all. I have included a few in the bibliography but a good search will usually let you find what you are looking for. (There is, for example, one site devoted to feminist mystery writers.)

If you live, work or receive healing in a setting such as a women's shelter, hospital, prison or rehabilitation centre, you may want to start a group there, where women on the margins of existence can begin telling their stories. Adolescents, in school and out, have also formed groups to do writing, theatre and film.

The CBC Connection

We have, in Canada, a way of connecting the country that began well before the Internet age. CBC Radio was one of the main ways I learned about different parts of Canada when I first came here to live. *Morningside* brought me items as varied as a speech by Trudeau and a recipe for Saskatchewan chili sauce. The radio is especially good at bringing to public attention the work of Canadian and worldwide writers, both new and established. Hearing the words aloud is often better than reading them, and it is fascinating to hear writers talk about their own work and their ways of working.

More and more programs encourage listeners to call, write or e-mail with their own stories. *This Morning* has the feature "First Person Singular." *Richardson's Round-up* is, in large part,

Opening Doors

built around listener's stories and comments: "Who taught you to make a nice cup of tea?" "What are your memories of Paris?" "Tell us a *ferry* story." What is wonderful about the *Round-up* is the way listeners respond to each other's stories. I once wrote in to tell how my old fear of driving over bridges stopped me in the middle of a Florida highway, after I'd heard another woman's story about her mother's fear of ferries in the Maritimes. When you begin writing on one topic you never know where the story will lead you. Other callers have started with knitting, and found themselves talking about the Second World War. These stories, heard all over Canada and parts of the United States, help us see what we all have in common. They show, too, that writing/telling does not have to be a vast project; we can stitch our lives together, a little at a time.

Readings

Readings are wonderful places to hear a writer's words in her or his own voice, to ask questions about the work and the writing process, and to get a sense of writers as people. Some poetry readings have open mikes where newcomers can read their own work. This is the time to dive in, risk the absurd, "just do it." Each reading is practice for the next one, and your words may touch someone in the audience in a special way. Remember, though, that open mike readings are meant to be short.

It helps to read out loud, at home, the pieces you plan to present at a reading: you get a sense of their rhythm, know when to pause, what to emphasize, and hear any lingering awkwardness. Sometimes I change the words unconsciously to a more easily spoken form, adding or omitting an "and," or changing a phrase. Reading aloud to each other during a writing group or workshop is good experience for future readings. When I teach in schools, I ask everyone to read aloud, but never force anyone. Sometimes a shy student will ask a friend to read her poem. Hearing your work read by someone else allows you to really listen to it, as if for the first time. When you

EVERYTHING ELSE

hear your words in someone else's voice, sometimes you see new things in the piece.

Writing "Give-aways"

Following one of Natalie Goldberg's suggestions, I have occasionally offered "one-minute poems" at fairs, bazaars and fundraising affairs, where people suggest a subject and I write a one-page poem on that topic. This is helpful practice both for beginners and for more experienced writers. Quick and spontaneous, without revision, these poems capture the thoughts of the moment. Writing on a suggested topic stretches your mind and can lead you to surprising discoveries. Finally, you give the poem away freely, not hanging onto it like a squirrel gathering nuts for winter. People often remind me about these poems; one woman told me she would frame the poem I wrote for her baby daughter and hang it on the child's wall.

Publication

This book is a guide to the writing process, not to publication, but here are a few thoughts. Publication, like reading in public, is a leap into the wider world. Some people look for ways to publish, others write only for themselves, and some people find themselves drawn into publication almost inadvertently. For example, there's a contest or a call for an anthology on exactly the subject you have been writing about for a while: grandmothers, or miscarriage, or old recipes, and you think about submitting your piece. Perhaps your school or workplace is putting together an anthology or magazine. These can be good opportunities for first publishing your work.

Keep in mind, however, that not every piece *should* be published. If you write a piece for yourself, it is successful if it gives you new insight, or makes you feel better, or expresses your feelings. The piece should be published only if it will work for others — a more demanding standard. The process of

Opening Doors

writing for publication is very different from writing for yourself, or for a class or writing group. You have to think rigorously about the revision process. You have to be willing to rethink some of your imagery, or even the structure of the piece as a whole; add or omit characters; look carefully at your use of language; perhaps cut a favourite section; and push the whole work that much further. This can be exciting and rewarding, but it is hard work. When writing appears to flow naturally and effortlessly, it often got that way through a great deal of time and effort.

You also have to be able to take advice or constructive criticism from others, to listen to different opinions and to think about what is useful and what is not. One teacher told me that you often need to cut the first page of a story, because the real beginning comes later. I have found this is good to keep in mind, but not always true. A good critique can help you notice habits that you've acquired along the way. For instance, I tended to use parentheses a great deal, until another writer I knew commented on this and wondered why I needed to apologize for my thoughts. Through revision and critique, you come to realize that your writing isn't you, although, of course, part of yourself goes into your work.

Once you've written and revised something that you want to see the light of day, how do you go about it? Usually it's best to start submitting poems and short stories to journals and magazines, rather than to try for a book right away. You need to find a periodical that publishes work somewhat in the same vein as yours and to find out whether it is accepting submissions. This information may be given in the periodical itself or in one of the writer's market guides, which you can probably find in your library.

There is a proper format for submissions: a short, businesslike letter summarizing what you are sending, a sample if you are sending a longer work and a self-addressed stamped envelope for response. Always make sure you keep a copy of

EVERYTHING ELSE

the piece for yourself, as well as a copy of your query letter. And steel yourself for plenty of rejection letters. When your work is rejected, it doesn't mean it isn't good; it just means it isn't what that editor is looking for right now. Editors sometimes offer suggestions or encouraging comments, but many don't have the time. More information on the submitting and publishing process can be found in some of the books in the "Further Reading" section at the end of this book.

Keep Reading!

Read, read, read! You may like some things more than others, but always you will become more aware of various people's writing styles and subject matter. It may inspire you, it will certainly give you new literary friends and companions. It's exciting to discover a writer, old or new, whom you have never met before. One good thing about knowing a second or third language is that the range of reading material is much wider, although excellent translations are also available. And if you know two or more languages, practising translation as a writing exercise is effective in sharpening your writing skills.

Read as widely as you can — mythology, history, science and technology, politics, biography, travel, sports, books on cooking, fashion, and gardening, published diaries and letters, as well as fiction and poetry. All this adds to your knowledge and wonder about the world and may inspire your own writing. Some writers have made writers from the past into characters in their own books. Margaret Atwood's book of poems *The Journals of Susannah Moodie* reinterprets Moodie's nineteenth-century memoirs about life in Canada. And Lorna Crozier has taken a fictional character, Mrs. Bentley of *As For Me and My House* by Sinclair Ross, and created a book of poems in her voice, *The Collected Poems of Mrs. Bentley*.

Opening Doors

And Keep Writing!

This book is based on the metaphor of directions in space and time, and gives some directions, practical and theoretical, to help you on your own way with writing. But there aren't always clear directions on the path of writing.

On a retreat in early winter, another woman and I went walking and saw three deer suddenly leap from behind some trees, disappearing uphill. As we walked along, we checked places where the deer might eat and bed down, and decided to return for another walk the next day at the same time. We had a good walk, but, of course, saw no deer.

As I thought about this, I realized that in old and modern works as different as Dante's *Divine Comedy* and Stephen Sondheim's musical *Into the Woods*, the woods are places where we lose all sense of direction. Because we have risked going into the woods, into the unknown, all kinds of terrible and wonderful things might happen.

And usually we do find our way out.

Writing practice is like walking in the woods. We might hope to see a deer, but that isn't the reason we walk. We just go for a walk, in all kinds of weather, sometimes with a friend, often alone. We get hot, we get cold and wet. We might see a deer the first day, then not again for weeks. We might see one only after many years. We certainly have a better chance if we go walking every day (even if we sometimes have to miss a day or two.) We learn to walk better, to see things around us like chickadees and dogtooth violets, little stones and lightning-struck trees. If a deer is there, our eyes are open to see it; we're in tune in the present, and not concentrating on tomorrow's supper or yesterday's fight.

"*How far can you go into the woods? Halfway, then you're going out again.*" Words from a friend's story that have stayed with me. But we never come out in exactly the same place we started from.

EVERYTHING ELSE

Last Words

Writing does mean spending some solitary time, but I don't think it means giving up ordinary life. The poet W.H. Auden advised writers to do other things, cook, garden, take care of animals, go hiking and canoeing. And, as one author noted, writing may have unexpected rewards. "Writing is wonderful. I lost my cow, wrote a story about it, and made enough money to buy another cow." Even if we don't make enough money to buy another cow, we might find someone who gives us a handful of magic beans. At least we get a good story.

Finally, a note about *poetic licence*. This term, I think, is both about the freedom to use language in a personal way and about the responsibility to use language with care. The more we write and live intimately with language, the less likely we are to use words in destructive or thoughtless ways and to be taken in by false claims, euphemisms, fuzzy thinking and attempts to manipulate our feelings, whether in advertising, politics, even the arts. And, most important, we can write from "a force field of love" and "do (our) work with joy."

❊

REFERENCES

Works Cited in Text

Alexander, Becky. *On Raven's Wing*. Cambridge, ON: Craigleigh Press, 2000.

Alvarez, Julia. "Naming the Fabrics." In *A Formal Feeling Comes: Poetry in Form by Contemporary Women*, Annie Finch, ed. Brownsville, OR: Story Line Press, 1994.

Atwood, Margaret. *The Journals of Susannah Moodie*. Toronto: Oxford University Press, 1970.

___. *Strange Things: The Malevolent North in Canadian Literaure*. Toronto: Oxford University Press, 1995.

Basho. Haiku, cited in *The Year of My Life*, a translation of Issa's "Oraga Haru," by Nobuyuki Yuasa. Berkeley: University of California Press, 1960.

Bateson, Mary Catherine. *Composing A Life*. New York: Atlantic Monthly Press, 1989.

Billy, Mary. Excerpt from "Giving Notice." *We'Moon Calendar, 2000*. Estacada, OR: Mother Tongue Ink, 2000. Poem previously published in *Over The Falls*, by Mary Billy. Squamish, BC: Herspectives Publishing, 1998.

Brecht, Bertold. *Galileo and Stories of Herr Keuner*, cited in *Brecht: A Biography*, by Ronald Hayman. New York: Oxford University Press, 1983.

Burroway, Janet. *Writing Fiction: A Guide to Narrative Craft*. 5th ed. Reading, MA: Addison-Wesley, 1999.

Butler, Sandra, and Barbara Rosenblum. *Cancer in Two Voices*. San Francisco: Spinsters Book Company, 1991.

Cameron, Anne. "The World is Full of Magic." In *Celebrating Canadian Women: Prose and Poetry By and About Women*, Greta Hofmann Nemiroff, ed. Toronto: Fitzhenry and Whiteside, 1989.

Cameron, Julia. *The Artist's Way*. New York: Jeremy P. Tarcher/Putnam, G.P. Putnam's Sons, 1992.

___. *The Right to Write: An Invitation and Initiation into the Writing Life*. New York: Jeremy P. Tarcher/Putnam, Penguin Putnam Inc., 1998.

Conrad, Joseph. *Lord Jim*. New York: Modern Library, 1921.

Crozier, Lorna. "Without Hands" and "Nothing Missing." *Angels of Flesh*,

Angels of Silence. Toronto: McClelland and Stewart, Inc., 1988.

___. *Saving Grace: The Collected Poems of Mrs. Bentley*. Toronto: McClelland and Stewart, 1996.

Danica, Elly. *Don't: A Woman's Word*. Charlottetown: gynergy books, 1988.

___. *Beyond Don't: Dreaming Past the Dark*. Charlottetown: gynergy books, 1996.

DaSalvo, Louise. *Writing As a Way of Healing: How Telling Our Stories Transforms Our Lives*. Boston: Beacon Press, 1999.

Dickinson, Emily. *The Complete Poems*. Thomas H. Johnson, ed. Boston, Toronto: Little Brown and Co., 1961.

Echlin, Kim. *Elephant Winter*. Toronto: The Penguin Group, 1997.

Edelman, Hope. *Motherless Daughters: The Legacy of Loss*. Reading, MA: Addison-Wesley Publishing Company, 1994.

Eliot, George. *Middlemarch*. New York: New American Library, 1964.

Engel, Marion. *Bear*. Toronto: McClelland and Stewart, 1984.

Esquivel, Laura. *Like Water for Chocolate*. New York: Anchor Books, 1994.

Estes, Clarissa Pinkola. *Women Who Run with the Wolves: Myths and Stories of the Wild Woman Archetype*. New York: Ballantine Books, 1992.

Finch, Annie, ed. *A Formal Feeling Comes: Poetry in Form by Contemporary Women*. Brownsville, OR: Story Line Press, 1994.

Forché, Carolyn. *Against Forgetting: Twentieth-Century Poetry of Witness*. New York: W.W. Norton and Co., 1993.

Frank, Anne. *The Diary of a Young Girl*. (The Definitive Edition.) Otto H. Frank and Mirjam Pressler, eds., translated by Susan Massotty. New York: Anchor Books/Doubleday, 1995.

Gilman, Charlotte Perkins, "The Yellow Wallpaper." In *Great Short Stories by American Women*. Candace Ward, ed. New York: Dover Publications, Inc, 1996.

Gilman, Phoebe. *Something from Nothing*. Richmond Hill, ON: Scholastic Canada, 1992.

Goldberg, Bonni. *Room to Write: Daily Invitations to a Writer's Life*. New York: Jeremy P. Tarcher/ Putnam, 1996.

Goldberg, Natalie. *Writing Down the Bones: Freeing the Writer Within*. Boston: Shambala, 1986.

Goldsmith, Diane. "Morning Musings." *We'Moon Calendar, 2000*. Estacada, OR: Mother Tongue Ink, 2000.

Gowdy, Barbara. *The White Bone*. Toronto: HarperFlamingoCanada, 1998.

Grahn, Judy. "A Woman is Talking to Death." *The Work of a Common Woman*. Freedom, CA: Crossing Press, 1972.

Gunn, Paula Allen, *The Sacred Hoop: Recovering the Feminine in American Indian Traditions*. Boston: Beacon Press, 1986.

Haight, Amanda. *Anna Akhmatova: A Poetic Pilgrimage*. New York: Oxford University Press, 1976.

Highway, Tomson. *Kiss of the Fur Queen*. Toronto: Doubleday Canada, 1998.

Hill, Barbara-Helen. *Shaking the Rattle*. Penticton, BC: Theytus Books Ltd., 1995.

Hogan, Linda, Deena Metzger, and Brenda Peterson, eds. *Intimate Nature: The Bond Between Women and Animals*. New York: Fawcett Columbine/The Ballantine Publishing Group, 1998.

I Never Saw Another Butterfly ... Children's Drawings and Poems from Theresienstadt. (Terezein) Concentration Camp, 1942-1944. New York: McGraw Hill Book Company, 1968.

Ingerman, Sandra. *Soul Retrieval: Mending the Fragmented Self*. San Francisco: HarperSanFrancisco, 1991.

Jaffe, Ellen. "Memory Kicks You in the Teeth Again." *Apparitions: Visions from the Millennium: Poetry of Lesley Chin Douglas, Ellen Jaffe, Gertrude Lebans*. Dundas, ON: artemis enterprises, 1997.

___, "On Loving Men in Difficult Times," "Requiem," "Roots," and "for Rose Albert," *Intricate Countries: Women Poets from Earth to Sky*. Dundas, ON: artemis enterprises, 1996.

James, Henry. *The Portrait of a Lady*. Oxford: Oxford University Press (World Classics Edition), 1981.

Jameson, Anna Brownell. *Winter Studies and Summer Rambles in Canada*. Toronto: Thomas Nelson and Sons, Ltd., 1943.

Kanter, Lynn. *On Lill Street*. Chicago: Third Side Press, 1992.

___. *The Mayor of Heaven*. Chicago: Third Side Press, 1998.

Khalsa, Dayal Kaur. *Cowboy Dreams*. New York: Clarkson N. Potter, 1990.

___. *Tales of a Gambling Grandma*. Montreal: Tundra Books, 1986.

Koch, Kenneth. *Wishes, Lies, and Dreams*. New York: Vintage, 1970.

Kogawa, Joy. *Obasan*. Toronto: Lester and Orpen Dennys, 1981; reprinted, Toronto: Doubleday, 1994.

Lamott, Anne. *Bird by Bird: Some Instructions on Writing and Life*. New York: Anchor Books, Doubleday, 1994.

Lane, Phil, Judie Bopp, Michael Bopp and Lee Brown. *The Sacred Tree*. Lethbridge, AB: Four Worlds Development Press, 1984.

Laurence, Margaret. *Jason's Quest*. Toronto: McClelland and Stewart, 1970.

___. *The Stone Angel*. Toronto: McClelland and Stewart, 1964.

Lawrence, Jacqueline. "My Five Moms." Ottawa: Talking Marigold, 2001.

Lebans, Gertrude. "Lake Joseph." *Intricate Countries: Women Poets from Earth to Sky.* Dundas, ON: artemis enterprises, 1996.

LeGuin, Ursula K. "The Fisherwoman's Daughter," and "Where Do You Get Your Ideas From?" *Dancing at the Edge of the World: Thoughts on Women, Words, Places.* New York: Grove Press, 1989.

___. "She Unnames Them." *Buffalo Gals and Other Animal Presences.* Santa Barbara: Capra Press 1987.

___. *The Left Hand of Darkness.* New York: Walker, 1968.

Lessing, Doris. *The Golden Notebook.* London: Michael Joseph, 1962.

Levertov, Denise. "Come Into Animal Presence." In Hogan et al., *Intimate Nature.* New York: Fawcett Columbine/The Ballantine Publishing Group, 1998.

Lewis, C.S. *The Narnia Chronicles.* New York: The Macmillan Company, 1950.

Li Ch'ing-chao, excerpt in *A Book of Women Poets from Antiquity to Now.* Aliki Barnstone and Willis Barnstone, eds. New York: Schocken Books, 1980.

Lorde, Audre. "The Transformation of Silence into Thought and Action" and "Uses of the Erotic." *Sister Outsider: Essays and Speeches.* Freedom, CA: Crossing Press, 1984.

Machado, Antonio. Stanza from "When I Lay Sleeping." *Times Alone,* trans. Robert Bly. Middletown: Wesleyan University Press, 1983.

McFadden, David. "The Night Watchman" and "Malcolm Lowry." *The Art of Darkness.* Toronto: McClelland and Stewart, 1984.

Mahler, Margaret, Fred Pines, and Anni Bergman. *The Psychological Birth of the Human Infant: Symbiosis and Individuation.* New York: Basic Books, 1975.

Meigs, Mary. *In The Company of Strangers.* Vancouver: Talon Books, 1991.

Michaels, Anne. *Fugitive Pieces.* Toronto: McClelland and Stewart, 1996.

Miedma, Baukje, Janet M Stoppard, and Vivienne Anderson, eds. *Women's Bodies/Women's Lives: Health, Well-Being and Body Image.* Toronto: Sumach Press, 2000.

Miller, Dusty. *Women Who Hurt Themselves: A Story of Hope and Understanding.* New York: Basic Books, 1995.

Miller, Katie. *Holy Writ: A Writer Reflects on Creation and Inspiration.* Erin, ON: The Porcupine's Quill, 2000.

Milner, Marion. (Originally published under the pen-name Joanna Fields.) *A Life of One's Own.* London: Chatto and Windus, 1934; reprinted, London: Virago Press, 1986.

Mitchell, W.O. *Who Has Seen The Wind?* Toronto: Macmillan Co. 1947.

Montgomery, Lucy Maude. *Anne of Green Gables*. Toronto: Oxford University Press, 1992.

___. *Emily of New Moon*. Toronto: Oxford University Press, 1985.

___. *Journals*. Toronto: Oxford University Press, 1985.

Morrison, Toni. *Beloved*. New York: Alfred A. Knopf, 1987.

Moyers, Bill. *The Language of Life: A Festival of Poets*. New York: Doubleday, 1995.

Munch, Robert. *The Paper Bag Princess*. Toronto: Annick Press, 1983.

Munro, Alice. "Spelling" and "Royal Beatings." *Who Do You Think You Are?* Toronto: MacMillan of Canada, 1978.

O'Hara, Frank. "A True Adventure of Talking to the Sun at Fire Island," *Selected Poems*. Donald Allen, ed. New York: Vintage Books, Random House, 1974.

Oliver, Mary. *A Poetry Handbook*. New York: Harcourt, Brace, and Company, 1994.

Pennebaker, James W. *Opening Up: The Healing Power of Confiding in Others*. New York: Avon Books, 1990.

Philips, Marlene Nourbese. "Burn Sugar." *Oxford Book of Stories by Canadian Women in English*. Rosemary Sullivan, ed. Toronto: Oxford University Press, 1999.

Piercy, Marge. "Rape poem." *Circles on the Water: Selected Poems*. New York: Alfred A. Knopf, 1994.

___. *He, She, and It*. New York: Alfred.A. Knopf, 1991.

Pilling, Marilyn Gear. *The Field Next to Love*. Hamilton, ON: Flying Turtle Press, 1997.

Plumwood, Val. "Being Prey," *UTNE Reader* 100 (July-August 2000). Minneapolis, MN: Lens Publishing Co. Inc.

Radomsky, Nellie. *Lost Voices: Women, Chronic Pain, and Abuse*. New York: Harrington Park Press, 1995.

Reed, Henry. "Lessons of the War: Naming of Parts." *A Map of Verona and Other Poems*. New York: Reynal and Hitchcock, 1947.

Reichl, Ruth. *Tender at the Bone: Growing Up at the Table*. New York: Broadway Books, 1998.

Reyher, Becky. *My Mother is the Most Beautiful Woman in the World*. New York, NY: Lothrop, Lee and Shepard Co., 1945.

Rich, Adrienne. *What Is Found There: Notebooks on Poetry and Politics*. New York: W. W. Norton and Co., 1993.

Rimbaud, Arthur. "Vowels." *Complete Works, Selected Letters*. Translated, introduction and notes by Wallace Fowlie. Chicago: University of Chicago

Press, 1966.

Roethke, Theodore. "The Waking." *The Waking: Poems 1933-53.* Garden City, NY: Doubleday, 1953.

Ross, Sinclair. *As For Me and My House.* Toronto: McCleeland and Stewart, 1989.

Rule, Jane. *Fictions and Other Truths: A Film About Jane Rule.* Produced by Rina Fraticelli, Great Jane Productions, 1994.

___. *Memory Board.* Toronto: MacMillan of Canada, 1987.

Russ, Joanna. *How to Suppress Women's Writing.* Austin: University of Texas Press, 1983.

Sagebear, Renee. "Quivering." *Bite Me.* Hamilton: Gearing Up Press, 1997.

Sarton, May. *A Reckoning.* New York: W.W. Norton and Co., 1978.

Schoemperlen, Diane. *In the Language of Love: A Novel in 100 Chapters.* Toronto: HarperCollins, 1994.

Schwartz, Delmore. "In Dreams Begin Responsibilities." *In Dreams Begin Responsibilities,* 1939.

Sewell, Anna. *Black Beauty.* New York: Grosset and Dunlop, 1945.

Shields, Carol. *Swann: A Mystery.* Don Mills, ON: Stoddart, 1987.

Smyth, Joshua. "Sharing One's Story: Translating Emotional Experiences into Words as a Coping Tool." In *Coping: The Psychology of What Works.* C.R. Snyder, ed. New York: Oxford University Press, 1999.

Sprelman, Roger. *You're So Fat: Exploring Ojibway Discourse.* Toronto: University of Toronto Press, 1998.

Stacy, M.B. "Paid in Full." *Intricate Countries: Women Poets from Earth to Sky.* Dundas, ON: artemis enterprises, 1996.

Stevens, Monica L. "Silent Tears." In *Shaking the Rattle,* Barbara-Helen Hill. Penticton, BC: Theytus Books, 1995.

Strunk, William Jr., and E.B. White, *The Elements of Style.* 3rd ed. New York: MacMillan Publishing Co., 1979.

Swan, Susan. *The Biggest Modern Woman of the World.* Toronto: Lester and Orpen Dennys, 1983.

Tannen, Deborah. *You Just Don't Understand: Women and Men in Conversation.* New York: Morrow, 1990.

Terr, Lenore. *Too Scared to Cry.* New York: Basic Books, 1990.

Tihanyi, Eva. "Somewhere." *Diviners* (Summer 2000).

Tobin, Jacqueline L., and Raymond G. Dobard. *Hidden in Plain View.* New York: Anchor Books/Random House, 1999.

Tolkien, J.R.R. *The Lord of the Rings.* London: HarperCollins, 1991.

Turner-Vesselago, Barbara. *Freefall: Writing Without a Parachute.* Toronto: The Writing Space, n.d.

Valle, Gina, ed. *Our Grandmothers, Ourselves: Reflections of Canadian Women.* Vancouver: Raincoast Books, 1999.

Van Tighem, Patricia. *The Bear's Embrace.* Vancouver: Greystone Books, 2000.

Vozenilek, Helen. *Loss of the Ground Note: Women Writing about the Loss of their Mother.* Los Angeles: Clothespin Fever Press, 1992.

Vonnegut, Kurt. *Slaughter-House Five.* New York: Dell, 1968.

Walker, Alice. *The Color Purple.* New York: Harcourt, Brace, Jovanovich, 1982.

White, E.B. *Charlotte's Web.* New York: Harper Trophy/HarperCollins, 1952.

Wiseman, Adele. *Crackpot.* Toronto: McClelland and Stewart, 1984.

___. *Memoirs of a Book-Molesting Childhood and Other Essays.* Toronto: Oxford University Press, 1987.

Wolkstein, Diane. *The Magic Orange Tree and Other Haitian Folktales.* New York: Schocken Books, 1980.

Woodman, Marion. *The Pregnant Virgin.* Toronto: Inner City Books, 1985.

Woolf, Virginia. *A Room of One's Own.* London: Hogarth Press, 1929; reprinted Granada Publishing Ltd., 1977.

Wooldridge, Susan Goldsmith. *Poem-Crazy: Freeing Your Life with Words.* New York: Three Rivers Press/Random House, 1996.

FURTHER READING

* books with writing exercises.

* Adams, Kathleen. *The Way of the Journal: A Journal Therapy Workbook for Healing.* Lutherville, Maryland: The Siddran Press, 1993.

Baldwin, Christina. *Life's Companion: Journal Writing as a Spiritual Quest.* New York: Bantam, 1991.

* Bender, Sheila. *Writing Personal Poetry: Creating Poems from Your Life Experiences.* Cincinatti: Writers' Digest Books, 1998.

Brant, Beth. *Writing As Witness: Essay and Talk.* Toronto: Womens Press, 1994.

Dillard, Annie. *The Writing Life.* New York: Harper and Row, 1989.

* Doane, Sharon. *New Beginnings: A Creative Writing Guide for Women Who Have Left Abusive Partners.* Seattle: Seal Press, 1996.

Grassroots Women's Collective. *Voicing Our Stories/Remaking Our Lives.* Toronto: Second Story Press, 1999; now available from Sumach Press, Toronto.

Green, Richard. *The Writing Experience: An Iroquois Guide to Written Storytelling.* Sanborn, NY: Ricara Features, 2000.

* Hagan, Kay Leigh. *Internal Affairs: A Journal-Keeping Workbook for Self-Intimacy.* San Francisco: HarperSanFrancisco, 1990.

* ____. *Prayers to the Moon: Exercises in Self-Reflection.* San Francisco: HarperSanFrancisco, 1991.

Haines, Dawn Denham, Susan Newcomer, and Jacqueline Raphael. *Writing Together: How to Transform Your Writing in a Writing Group.* New York: The Berkeley Group/Penguin Putnam Inc., 1997.

* Newman, Leslea C. *Writing from the Heart: Inspiration and Exercises for Women Who Want to Write.* Freedom, CA: The Crossing Press, 1993.

Rae, Arlene Perly. *Everybody's Favourites: Canadians Talk about Books that Changed Their Lives.* Toronto: Penguin Books, 1997.

* Schiwy, Marlene. *A Voice of Her Own: Women and the Journal-Writing Journey.* New York: Simon and Schuster, 1996.

Sternburg, Janet, ed. *The Writer on Her Work.* New York: W.W. Norton and Company, 2000.

Truitt, Anne. *Daybook: The Journal of an Artist*. New York: Penguin, 1982.

____. *Turn: The Journal of an Artist*. New York: Viking, 1986.

Warland, Betsy. *Bloodroot: Tracing the Untelling of Motherloss*. Toronto: Second Story Press, 2000; now available from Sumach Press, Toronto.

A Few Internet Sources

1. Canadian Poetry
www.library.utoronto.ca/canpoetry
Information about poets, journals, presses, literary events, awards and contests, as well as links to poetry courses and other Canadian and international sites.

2. Canadian Authors' Association
http://www.canauthors.org/links/writing.html
Links to a wide variety of writing groups and associations (e.g., crime writers, children's authors, newsletters, information about writing services and courses).

3. Yahoo Women's Site for Arts, Humanities and Literature
http://ca.dir.yahoo.com/arts/humanities/literature/cultures_and_ groups/women/
Links to Canadian and international sites for women's writing, authors, publications, etc.

PERMISSIONS

Grateful acknowledgment is made for permission to reprint the following:

Becky Alexander, *On Raven's Wing* (excerpt). Copyright 2000 by Becky Alexander. Reprinted by permission of the author.

Mary Billy, excerpt from "Giving Notice," *Over The Falls*. Copyright 1999 by Mary Billy. Excerpt appeared in *We'Moon Calendar 2000*. Reprinted by permission of the author.

Richard Douglass Chin, "Market Day," *Apparitions: Visions from the Millennium*. artemis enterprises. Copyright 1997 by Richard Douglass Chin. Reprinted with the permission of the author.

Barbara Crooker, excerpt from "Starving for the Gold," originally published in *Aethlon*, 1998. Copyright 1998 by Barbara Crooker. Reprinted with the permission of the author.

"Without Hands" and excerpt from "Nothing Missing," *Angels of Flesh, Angels of Silence*, by Lorna Crozier. Copyright 1988 by Lorna Crozier. Used by permission of McClelland and Stewart, The Canadian Publishers.

Diane Goldsmith, "Morning Musings – Journal Excerpt," *We'Moon Calendar 2000*. Copyright 2000 by Diane Goldsmith. Reprinted by permission of the author.

Ellen Jaffe, "Requiem," and excerpts from "Roots" and "For Rose Albert," *Intricate Countries: Women Poets from Earth to Sky*. artemis enterprises. Copyright 1996 by Ellen Jaffe. Reprinted with permission of the author. Excerpt from "Memory Kicks You in the Teeth Again," *Apparitions: Visions from the Millennium*. artemis enterprises. Copyright 1997 by Ellen Jaffe. Reprinted with permission of the author.

Gertrude Lebans, "Lake Joseph," *Intricate Countries: Women Poets from Earth to Sky*. artemis enterprises, 1996. Copyright 1996 by Gertrude Lebans. Reprinted with the permission of the author.

Ursula K. LeGuin, excerpts from "The Fisherwoman's Daughter" and "Where Do You Get Your Ideas From?" in *Dancing at the Edge of the World*. Grove Press, 1989. Copyright 1989 by Ursula K. Leguin. Reprinted with the permission of Grove/Atlantic Inc.

Audre Lorde, excerpts from "The Transformation of Silence into Thought and Action" and "Uses of the Erotic," both published in *Sister Outsider*. Freedom, CA: The Crossing Press. Copyright 1984 by Audre Lorde. Reprinted with permission of The Crossing Press.

David McFadden. Excerpts from "The Night Watchman" and "Malcolm

Lowry," *The Art of Darkness*, McClelland and Stewart. Copyright 1984 by David McFadden. Reprinted by permission of the author.

Sandra McPherson, excerpt from interview with Bill Moyers in *The Language of Life: Poetry*. Bantam, Doubleday, Dell Publishing Group, Inc. Copyright 1995, by Bill Moyers. Reprinted by the permission of Bantam, Doubleday, Dell Publishing Group, Inc., a division of Random House.

Antonio Machado, stanza from "When I Lay Sleeping," *Times Alone*, translated by Robert Bly. Wesleyan University Press, Middletown, Connecticut. Copyright 1983, by Robert Bly. Reprinted by permission of Robert Bly.

Excerpts from "Spelling" and "Royal Beatings" from *Who Do You Think You Are?* by Alice Munro. Originally published in Canada by Macmillan of Canada. Copyright 1978 by Alice Munro. Reprinted by permission of William Morris Agency, Inc., on behalf of the Author.

Marilyn Gear Pilling, excerpt from "The Field Next to Love," *The Field Next to Love*. Turtle Press. Copyright 2000 by Marilyn Gear Pilling. Reprinted by permission of the author.

Jane Rule, quotes from the film *Fiction and Other Truths: A Film about Jane Rule*, produced by Rina Fraticelli, 1995. Permission to use quotes granted by Jane Rule and by Rina Fraticelli.

Renee Sagebear, "Quivering," *Bite Me*. Gearing Up Press. Copyright 1997 by Renee Sagebear. Reprinted by permission of the author.

M.B. Stacy, "The Scar Clan," *Intricate Countries: Women Poets from Earth to Sky*. artemis enterprises. Copyright 1996 by M.B. Stacy. Reprinted by permission of the author.

Monica Stevens, "Silent Tears," published in *Shaking the Rattle*, by Barbara-Helen Hill. Theytus Press. Copyright 1995 by Barbara-Helen Hill. Reprinted by permission of Monica Stevens and Barbara-Helen Hill.

Eva Tihanyi, excerpt from "Somewhere" *Diviners*, Summer 2000. Copyright 2000 by Eva Tihanyi. Reprinted by permission of the author.

Susan Goldsmith Wooldridge, excerpts from Chapter 14, "full moon me," *Poem Crazy: Freeing Your Life with Words*. Copyright 1996 by Susan Goldsmith Wooldridge. Reprinted by permission of Carol Southern Books, a division of Random House, Inc.

Grateful acknowledgment is also made for permission to reprint the following unpublished material:

Linda Marie Fulcher, "Cliff Avenue." Copyright 2000 by Linda Marie Fulcher.

Angela Hrabowiak, "Secrets." Copyright 2001 by Angela Hrabowiak.

Sandra Kenny, excerpt from "Winter's Diary." Copyright 1999 by Sandra Kenny.

Morgan Combe, "Where Have We Met Before?" Copyright 2000 by Morgan Combe.

Gina Shelton, "Seasons" and "Dyku." Copyright 2000 by Gina Shelton.

Every effort has been made to trace all the copyright holders, but if any have been inadvertently overlooked the publisher will be pleased to make the necessary arrangement at the first opportunity.